TREE FLOWERS
OF
FOREST, PARK, AND STREET

By

WALTER E ROGERS

Late Professor of Botany in Lawrence College

THE DRAWINGS FROM NATURE

by

OLGA A. SMITH

Instructor in Botany in Lawrence College

DOVER PUBLICATIONS, INC.
NEW YORK

Published in Canada by General Publishing Company, Ltd., 30 Lesmill Road, Don Mills, Toronto, Ontario.
Published in the United Kingdom by Constable and Company, Limited, 10 Orange Street, London W.C.2.

This Dover edition, first published in 1965, is an unabridged republication of the work first published by the author in 1935, to which has been added a memorial dedication prepared especially for this Dover edition.

Library of Congress Catalog Card Number: 65-13152

Manufactured in the United States of America

Dover Publications, Inc.
180 Varick Street
New York 14, N.Y.

TO

N. M. R.

REPUBLICATION of this book is an especially satisfying event, for
a number of reasons. First, it is a tribute to its author, the late
Walter E Rogers, and the diligent effort he expended over so
many years to see his project come to press the first time. In
addition, this reissue will make it possible for many more people
to enjoy the beauty of tree flowers.

The original work took shape slowly in the author's mind as
he collected photographs of tree flowers over a long period of
years. More intensive preparation immediately preceded the
actual publication. But when publication was finally decided
upon, the depression had descended, and no publishing company
would risk the large expenses connected with the sort of volume
envisioned. The author's personal management and financing
of the entire operation took a good deal of courage and faith at
that time. Financial security in every form was risked to back
the publication costs. Thus, the book was a true labor of love.

The general advice of people experienced in publishing indicated that an edition of only 750 copies was likely to be "safe."
But on the advice of a single person whose judgment was
respected, an edition twice that size was finally printed. Within
four years the printing was exhausted; nevertheless, orders continued to come in, unsolicited, in numbers that were satisfying,
yet disturbing since they could not be filled. The present republication makes the book available to an extent that could only
be dreamed of at the time of initial publication.

Although meeting the heavy demands of a teaching schedule
in a small college, Walter Rogers left behind two major professional heritages: this work, and the students about whom he
cared so much, some of whose later academic and professional
careers delighted him in his last years.

In addition to the original dedication to his wife, Nellie
Martin Rogers, a rededication should include Walter Rogers
himself.

K. T. R.

TABLE OF CONTENTS

INTRODUCTION

DESPITE the fact that trees are flowering plants as truly as are lilies or roses, few people outside the ranks of habitual observers of nature are familiar with the flowers of trees. Indeed the very existence of such flowers, excepting those of commercial fruit trees and of a few showy ornamentals, is scarcely known, and one of the most widely prevalent ideas concerning trees is that they are plants which do not produce flowers.

That tree flowers are not well known is due primarily to the fact that they are seldom of large size and so do not attract attention to themselves as do the showier blossoms of the herbs found in our gardens, conservatories, and woodlands. All tree flowers are, however, large enough to be easily seen by the naked eye and the smallest of them can be satisfactorily studied with the aid of a simple lens. Many of them are of exquisite form. Some are equalled in brilliance of coloring by only the most gorgeous of our hothouse plants, while others are unexcelled in delicacy of both form and color. Without question, many of our native trees would be cultivated principally for their flowers were these somewhat larger in size.

THE PLATES

With the idea in mind of representing the small flowers of trees on a scale large enough to make them seem comparable in size with more commonly known flowers, the writer devised a special technique by means of which such objects could be photographed six to twelve times their natural dimensions. The image obtained by this method was then still further enlarged in the process of making a half-tone, so that the final magnification of the object is, in some cases, twenty to thirty times the original size. In this manner, even floral features which are almost indistinguishable to the unaided eye could be brought up to the point of easy visibility. In most cases the natural size of the subject has been indicated by a drawing at the top of the title page which accompanies the plate, and the extent of magnification is therefore obvious.

[viii]

Three quarters of the plates of the book were produced by the method outlined above. The remaining quarter were obtained by ordinary methods of photography. Some of the latter have been inserted for the purpose of affording settings for the subjects of other plates, but most of them have been added for the purpose of making a more representative series.

In the selection of forms for photographing the attempt was made to give representation to as many important plant families as possible. A few families which should have been represented had to be omitted because of failure to obtain materials suitable for photographic purposes. It should be understood that the selection of forms within a family was made in a purely arbitrary manner. The use of the Maples to illustrate stages in the opening of winter buds and of individual flower buds was also arbitrary, and doubtless another type would have been just as satisfactory.

A number of people have expressed disappointment in the fact that the plates were not to be rendered in natural colors. The technical difficulties to be encountered in adapting any existing color process to the portrayal of tree flowers would be enormous, and it is the opinion of the writer that at present it is not possible to give a true rendition of the colors of many of these structures.

In connection with the plates it should be stated that while backgrounds and accessory features were somewhat altered in a number of cases, in only two instances did the floral subjects themselves receive retouching treatment. One of these was the case of the Waahoo flower. In the course of magnification, the mottling of the petals was so accentuated as to make the flower appear altogether unnatural, and the effect had to be softened. The second case was that of the Persimmon. Circumstances had forced the photographing of a flower, the petals of which were discolored, and the latter had to be lightened. It is believed that in the process of retouching these two subjects, the engraver has almost entirely avoided artificial effects.

THE TEXT

No attempt has been made to write technical descriptions of the flowers and flower-clusters which are portrayed in the plates. Those desiring such descriptions should consult Sargent's

*Manual of the Trees of North America.** While offering briefer treatments, Britton and Brown's *Illustrated Flora of the Northern States and Canada*, Small's *Manual of the Southeastern Flora*, and Gray's *New Manual of Botany*, are highly useful. The writer has drawn freely from these authorities, and it would be impossible for him to acknowledge specifically his indebtedness to each.

The book is intended to be and is chiefly pictorial. Text matter has been included for the purpose, in some cases, of explaining features of plates that might not be pictorially self-explanatory; of providing, in other cases, a background of more or less well known facts against which the photograph may be better comprehended; and of presenting, in still other cases, certain relevant and accessory facts which are of interest in connection with the flower.

The informed reader will look in vain for anything new in the text. A critical eye will find, as the pages are turned, neither continuity nor consistency of treatment. It should be borne in mind that, except in cases where a series such as the Elms or the Maples was being considered, each plate was treated independently of all others.

THE SCIENTIFIC NAMES

The scientific names are those of Gray's Manual. The system of that manual was departed from in two instances; once, when the Elms and the Mulberries were placed in families of their own, instead of together in the Nettle Family; and again, when the Horse-chestnut Family was separated from the Soapberry Family. Precedent for both of these changes may be found in other manuals.

THE SILHOUETTES

During an experience in teaching plant science which has extended over a period of more than twenty years, two things connected with the relations of humans to trees have impressed themselves with peculiar emphasis on the mind of the writer.

One is the almost universal lack of knowledge of the fact that our common trees are flowering plants. The photography represented in this book was undertaken and pursued with that lack of knowledge in mind.

* Republished by Dover Publications, Inc., in 1961.

The second is the very general lack of appreciation of trees as components of the winter landscape. It is true that there is, on the part of many people, considerable appreciation of trees in the summer condition. But for half of the year most trees are leafless, and in this condition they receive scant attention. Now, as a matter of fact, it is when defoliated that the tree displays many of its most interesting characters. The outline of the whole plant, the extent to which the main axis of the tree is conserved in the crown, the manner of branching, the angle of subsidiary branch with its primary, the abundance and size of ultimate branchlets—in fact almost everything that could be included in what we might call the general artistic anatomy of the tree shows up to advantage in the winter condition, whereas in summer these features are more or less completely cloaked under a canopy of foliage.

All the features mentioned above vary more or less with the kind of tree, and are, in general, distinctive for each species. This is not to state that there is no variation between individuals of a kind; on the contrary, there is a great deal of it, but it is true as a generality that each tree species has its own anatomical pattern, which if shared at all with others, is shared only with close relatives. The observation or study of these patterns is properly a matter for winter activity, and it was with the idea of attempting to stimulate interest in the winter aspects of trees that the silhouettes were drawn for this volume.

The book then, has as its two purposes; first, the calling of attention to the existence of tree flowers and the portrayal of some of their variations, and second, the stimulation of interest in the winter characteristics of trees. If it seems that these two objectives have been brought together by violence, the only reply which the author can make is that both appear to him worthwhile, and neither appears to have received enough emphasis in the literature dealing with trees.

THE MARGINAL DRAWINGS

As stated previously, the small drawing which is placed above the plate title on many of the text pages is intended to show the natural size of the flower which appears on the plate. The drawings on the margins of the text pages are intended to present some interesting and distinctive features of the tree, and should assist materially in helping the reader to associate the flower represented with the plant to which it belongs.

ACKNOWLEDGMENTS

For encouragement in the effort to bring out this book I owe much to the following individuals: Dr. H. A. Gleason, of the New York Botanical Garden, Dr. E. D. Merrill, of Harvard University. Dr. C. Stuart Gager, of the Brooklyn Botanic Garden, Dr. S. T. Dana, of the University of Michigan, Dr. Aven Nelson, of the University of Wyoming, Dr. E. E. Sherff, of the Chicago Normal College, Dr. Edgar Anderson, of the Missouri Botanical Garden, and Dr. H. C. Hanson, of the North Dakota Agricultural College.

To my sister, Mrs. Arthur O'Keefe, who has, over a period of several years, sent me material from the Sangamon valley of Illinois, I am very grateful. Mr. Herman A. Howard of the Arnold Arboretum has, with the greatest care, collected and forwarded to me various materials, and to him and to the authorities of the Arboretum I extend hearty thanks. Dr. George T. Moore and the staff of the Missouri Botanical Garden have generously sent me specimens, and the favor is hereby acknowledged. While in the Great Smoky Mountains National Park, I was permitted to collect a limited amount of material, and for that privilege I have to thank Superintendent J. R. Eakin.

The photographic work was greatly facilitated by the efforts of Mr. Frank Koch who, no matter how busy, could always find time to develop a negative or furnish a quick proof. In the matter of paper and printing I have had the advice of Mr. E. G. Colvin. To both Mr. Koch and Mr. Colvin I wish to express my thanks.

For invaluable aid in the preparation of the manuscript I am indebted to my daughters Mary and Julia.

To Mr. George Banta of the Collegiate Press and to Mr. C. C. Thomas, of Springfield, Illinois, I owe much for advice relative to publishing. The officers and staffs of both the Appleton Engraving Company, and the Collegiate Press have been, to the fullest possible extent, kindly coöperative in helping me to realize the original plans for the book.

Finally I wish to express my undying gratitude to Mr. S. F. Shattuck, that long admired friend who, by his generous financial support, has made it possible to take the book to press.

MAIDENHAIR TREE

Seed-bearing Flower
MAIDENHAIR TREE
Ginkgo biloba L.

MAIDENHAIR TREE FAMILY   GINKGOACEAE

In the minds of those who invariably associate the term "flower" with showy color display and certain patterns of form, the idea that this simple object from the Maidenhair Tree is a flower may not find ready acceptance. But it does no violence to the definition of the term to regard this structure as a true flower. It is, of course, exceedingly simple. It shares with the corresponding structure of the Cycads the distinction of being probably the simplest flower of any of the seed-bearing plants. There is no calyx and no corolla. The stamens are borne elsewhere; indeed, on another tree. Even the pistil is lacking, or is represented by only a rudimentary structure. However, in spite of the absence of these features, the true floral character is evidenced by the presence of ovules which eventually develop into seeds. From one to four of these are borne on an elongate axis, and the two represented in the plate are at a stage just ready to receive the fertilizing pollen from stamen-bearing flowers of another tree. This flower, then, may be said to be in full bloom.

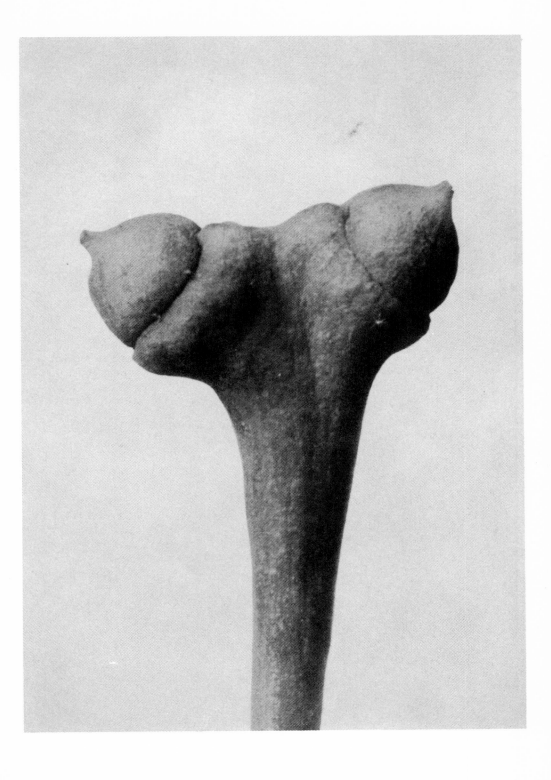

WHITE PINE

[5]

Seed-bearing Flower
WHITE PINE
Pinus strobus L.

PINE FAMILY   PINACEAE

In regions where the White Pine grows, mature seed cones of the tree are common objects. But the flowers from which the cones develop are rarely seen, even by students of plant life, for they occur typically only on the upper branches of more or less mature trees. Sometimes the twig tip bears two flowers; in other instances only one. Each flower consists of numerous ovule-bearing scales attached to a central axis. At the time of blooming, the color is light green, or reddish, or red; in any case the latter hue becomes dominant soon after pollination.

Following pollination, the flower, instead of wilting, expands somewhat and its scales toughen, so that by the end of the growing season it has become a bullet-shaped cone, one half to three quarters of an inch in length. Not until the end of the second season does it mature seeds. By that time the scales have become thick and woody, and the cone has expanded to a length of several inches. At maturity, the scales are drawn apart, and from between them the winged seeds drop out, to be whirled off on autumn winds.

WHITE PINE

Staminate Flowers
WHITE PINE
Pinus strobus L.

PINE FAMILY   PINACEAE

In their distribution on the trees, the pollen-bearing flowers of the White Pine are not so restricted as the seed-bearing, but neither are they so restricted in numbers.

Each flower consists of numerous stamens, the anthers being almost without stalks and densely aggregated on a central axis, the whole having much the form of a blackberry fruit. Each anther is comprised of two pollen sacs, and as the contained pollen ripens, the color of the flower changes from green to yellow. When the pollen sacs split open, the powdery pollen is exposed in such profusion as to obscure all details of structure. So enormous is the production of pollen by the Pine that during the time the tree is in flower, veritable clouds of the yellow grains may be seen floating away from its branches.

RED PINE

Seed-bearing Flowers
RED PINE
Pinus resinosa Ait.

PINE FAMILY   PINACEAE

The seed-bearing flowers of the Red Pine are characteristically borne in pairs at the tips of new shoots, and may occur at almost any elevation on the tree. Broadly egg-shaped or elliptical in outline, they are deep red in color and offer a pleasing contrast in both form and color, with the new, light green needles.

The short, compact character of the flower is retained as development into the mature cone proceeds, and the resulting structure is very different in form from the seed-cone of the White Pine.

The opening of the cones for release of the seeds does not, as in the case of the opening of a pea pod, involve the actual disruption of tissue, for the seeds lie free on the inner surfaces of the cone scales, and the scales are attached individually to the axis but not to one another. This character is common to all the members of the Pine Family, and because of it they, with others, are known as Gymnosperms, which means naked-seeded plants.

[14]

TAMARACK

Staminate Flowers

TAMARACK

Larix laricina (Du Roi) Koch.

PINE FAMILY   PINACEAE

To anyone who has known, as representatives of the cone-bearing trees, only
Pines, Spruces, Cedars, and the like, the
Tamarack is a very surprising tree. It has
the growth habit and the foliage of an
evergreen, but it sheds its leaves in the
autumn, and stands through the winter
as bare as any broad-leafed tree of the
forest. One professional botanist of the
past generation was fond of slyly calling
the Tamarack "a deciduous evergreen."

One must go into the low grounds early
in the season if he wishes to see the flowering of this tree. In the northern states it
is the earliest of the coniferous trees to
bloom.

The stamen-bearing flowers occur at
the ends of leafless, dwarf branches, and
consist of a number of stamens, only the
anthers of which can be seen, for the axis
of the cluster and the bases of the stamens
are hidden by a ring of persistent bud
scales; these crowd the stamens into a
compact rounded dome. The flowers at
maturity are yellow. After pollen discharge, the empty anthers, now straw
colored, remain in position on the twig
and weather off only tardily.

LARCH

Seed-bearing Flower

LARCH

Larix decidua Mill.

PINE FAMILY   PINACEAE

In contrast with the staminate structures of the Larch, the seed-bearing flowers occur at the tips of leafy shoots, and
their expansion just precedes that of the
leaves. They are cylindric in form, deep
red in color, and wax-like in texture. This
flower of the Larch is surpassed in beauty
by no other among all the Gymnosperms.
But those who hold strictly to the utili-
tarian explanation of floral colors must
be hard put to account for the gorgeous
color display of this flower, for the Larch,
in common with other Gymnosperms, is
strictly wind-pollinated, and its color can
have nothing to do with attracting insects.

In the development of the flower into
the seed-cone there are two points of
sharp difference between this case and
that of the Pine. The first is that the
Larch flower only doubles its dimensions
while that of the Pine increases enormously in size. The second is that the
Larch matures its seeds in one season,
while the Pine requires two.

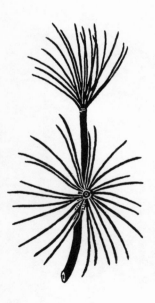

BLACK SPRUCE

Seed-bearing Flowers
BLACK SPRUCE
Picea mariana (Mill.) BSP.

PINE FAMILY   PINACEAE

Because it is so often used as a Christmas tree, the Black Spruce, to a large section of our population, is perhaps better known than any other evergreen. One of the features that makes the tree attractive as a holiday ornament is the usual occurrence of the seed-cones on the upper branches, and this is often true of quite small trees. The cones, when open and dry, are almost globular in shape. The surprisingly large number of cones which may be borne on one tree is due to the fact that after seed discharge they are almost indefinitely persistent; Professor Sargent states that they may remain on the tree for as long as twenty or thirty years. Since the numbers are added to with recurrent flowering, it is not to be wondered at that the trees sometimes appear to be heavily loaded with cones.

At the time of flowering, the cone is rather delicate. It displays a rich purplish red color which changes to brown before the seeds are ripe at the end of the season.

WHITE SPRUCE

Staminate Flower

WHITE SPRUCE

Picea canadensis (Mill.) BSP.

PINE FAMILY   PINACEAE

Just before the Spruce comes into bloom, the tree may be seen with scores of its twigs tipped by flaming red cones which are soon to release pollen. To those who are accustomed to think of the Spruce as just another evergreen, monotonously displaying the same color from one year's end to another, the tree at this period is very surprising.

As the conical flower expands, a suggestion of gold begins to creep in about the edges of the shield-like scale tips which completely encase the whole structure. As the full blooming stage arrives, the stamens separate, due to elongation of the central axis. Then the two anther sacs of each stamen split longitudinally, and the flood of light golden pollen is released to drift off in veritable showers on the air.

BALSAM FIR

Young Seed-bearing Cones
BALSAM FIR
Abies balsamea (L.) Mill.

PINE FAMILY   PINACEAE

Most desirable of the evergreens for use as Christmas trees are the firs. This preference is due not only to the superior form of the tree, but also to the fact that the leaves remain firmly attached even though the tree dries out completely. How much more desirable the tree would be if the cones were retained, probably few people know. But the cones normally shed their scales soon after the seeds mature, and as this occurs in the autumn following flowering, it is very unusual for the cones to be intact as late as the holiday season, though the central axis may long persist upright on the twig.

For beauty of form, regularity of scale arrangement, and softness of coloring, the seed-bearing cones of the fir are unsurpassed. Often their arrangement on the branches is such as to give the effect of tapers on a candelabrum. In the Balsam, this effect is heightened by the fact that the flowers occur only on the uppermost branches of the tree. Just at the stage of blooming, the cones (flowers) are somewhat different in appearance from those shown in the plate. At that time the scales are shorter than the pointed bracts, one of which stands just below each scale, and the whole structure presents a somewhat bristly appearance. But after pollination, the scales enlarge much more rapidly than the bracts, and the latter are soon lost from view.

HEMLOCK

Staminate Flower
HEMLOCK
Tsuga canadensis (L.) Carr.

PINE FAMILY   PINACEAE

The pollen-bearing flowers of the Hemlock are typically produced from buds in the axils of the previous season's leaves, but they sometimes appear as terminal on the twigs. Neither they nor the seed-bearing flowers are segregated in position, and a mature tree may display them on lower branches as well as upper. Blooming occurs before the new leaves of the season have developed.

The individual flower is more or less globular in form and in late development is thrust out of the scaly cup of the bud on the end of a stalk which lifts it out into an exposed position. Comprising the flower are less than a score of anthers, each globular in form, but flattening beneath as the two pollen sacs split open and release their contents. Though the flowers are small, their large numbers make for the production of a great quantity of pollen by the individual tree.

YOUNG HEMLOCK

Seed-bearing Flower
HEMLOCK
Tsuga canadensis (L.) Carr.

PINE FAMILY   PINACEAE

The Hemlock presents a seed-bearing flower that exhibits a marked difference from the Spruce in the fact that the color offers no sharp contrast with the foliage. The green is lighter than the green of the leaves, but the flowers do not stand out from their surroundings.

At the time of blooming, the flowers appear erect at the tips of the twigs, and in this position offer easy opportunity for pollen from the air to settle between the scales and gravitate downward to the beaks of the ovules, which face the central axis. Later the developing cones change color and position. When ready to shed their seeds at the end of the season, they are brown in hue and hang pendulous from the branch tips. The Hemlock cone is one of the smallest of the true cones, and because of its miniature size and its perfection of form, it rarely fails to attract interested attention from an observer.

ARBOR VITAE

Seed-bearing Flowers
ARBOR VITAE
Thuja occidentalis L.

PINE FAMILY   PINACEAE

Among the flowers of the Gymnosperms the extreme of inconspicuousness
is reached in the case of the Arbor Vitae,
or White Cedar. Not only is the color of
the flower practically identical with that
of the foliage, but the form and arrangement of the floral parts so closely resembles that of the adjacent leaves that the
flower appears to be merely a somewhat
swollen tip of a leafy branch. An inspec-
tion of the plate will reveal three of the
four rows of scales on each twig, and the
continuation of the rows into the tips.
Along the twigs these scales have a purely
vegetative function and are true leaves,
but at the tips of the side shoots, the
scales bear ovules on the lower ends of
the inner faces. They are, therefore, floral
parts.

After the flower has matured, the
nature of the parts is more evident, for
the cone which develops, while having
characteristic peculiarities of its own, is
still obviously a Gymnosperm cone.

The staminate flowers resemble to a
considerable extent those of the Hemlock, but are smaller, and are terminal.

RED CEDAR

Seed-bearing Flowers
RED CEDAR
Juniperus virginiana L.

PINE FAMILY   PINACEAE

Among the Gymnosperms, the Red Cedar, next after the Ginkgo, offers perhaps the flower hardest to recognize as such. The lack of a strongly differentiating color, the minuteness of the parts, the apparent similarity to foliage—all conspire to conceal from an observer the true nature of these flowers.

Borne at the tip of a short branch, or sometimes laterally, the flower consists of several fleshy scales, each bearing one or two ovules on its inner face. The upper ends of these ovules are openly exposed; this peculiarity is shared with only one other form which is described in this book, that is, the Ginkgo. Curiously enough, the maturing of the cone not only results in fusing the scales into a globular fleshy "berry," but the ovules are completely overgrown in the process and all external indication of their presence is lost. The color of the mature cone is deep blue.

[50]

RED CEDAR

[53]

Staminate Flowers
RED CEDAR
Juniperus virginiana L.

PINE FAMILY   PINACEAE

Only occasionally are the pollen-bearing flowers of Red Cedar produced on the same tree with the seed-bearing. Much more conspicuous to the eye than the latter, their brownish color apparently changes to creamy-yellow while the pollen is being shed. The flowers are terminal on short lateral shoots and often occur in such numbers as to give the appearance of completely loading the tree. Few other flowers of Gymnosperms create so definite an impression of orderliness as this. The number of stamens is usually ten or twelve, and these are arranged in four longitudinal rows and spaced with great exactness. The tip of each stamen axis is expanded into a circular shield, facing outward, and below this are the pollen sacs, of which there may be as many as six per stamen, an unusually high number among the flowers of our common evergreens.

[54]

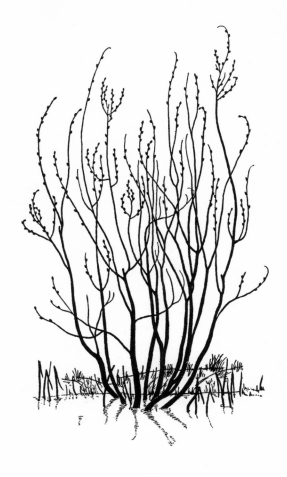

WILLOW

Winter Bud
WILLOW
Salix sp. (Tourn.) L.

WILLOW FAMILY   SALICACEAE

Trees which flower early in the year are under the necessity of preparing early for the occasion. Of necessity, most of this preparation occurs during the previous growing season, and often the flowers are fully developed, except in the matter of size, several months before they are to bloom.

To tide the newly formed floral parts through the austere winter season some sort of protective device is necessary. In the Willows, this covering consists of a single scale, which is in reality a leaf, highly modified to serve a protective, instead of a nutritive function. Though thin, this simple wrapping is highly waterproof and affords adequate protection against evaporation losses, which usually constitute in winter the most serious enemy of plants.

Willow buds which do not contain flowers, but only vegetative parts, are usually easy to recognize, for they lack the size and plumpness of flower buds.

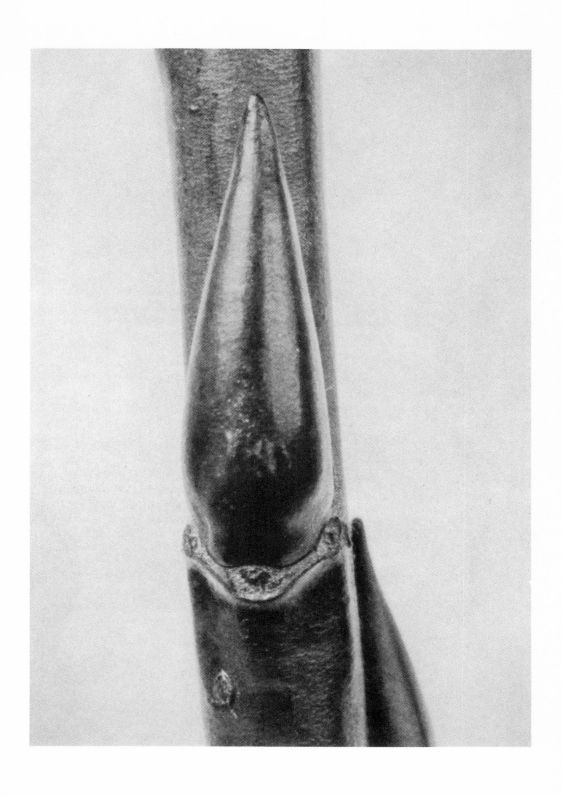

WILLOW

Opening Bud
WILLOW
Salix sp. (Tourn.) L.

WILLOW FAMILY   SALICACEAE

One of the early signs of spring's return each year is the opening of the buds of the Willow.

Within the conical waterproof tent of the Willow bud lies an unexpanded flower-cluster, or inflorescence. Normally the inflorescence escapes from its winter covering by expanding to the point where the overlapping scale edges are forced apart, and as the cluster grows, the scale itself is gradually pushed aside until finally its connection with the stem is so weakened that it falls off. The plate illustrates a case that is somewhat abnormal, but one which is frequently seen when winter twigs are cut and brought inside. Then often the scale loosens at the base and works up over the tip of the axis.

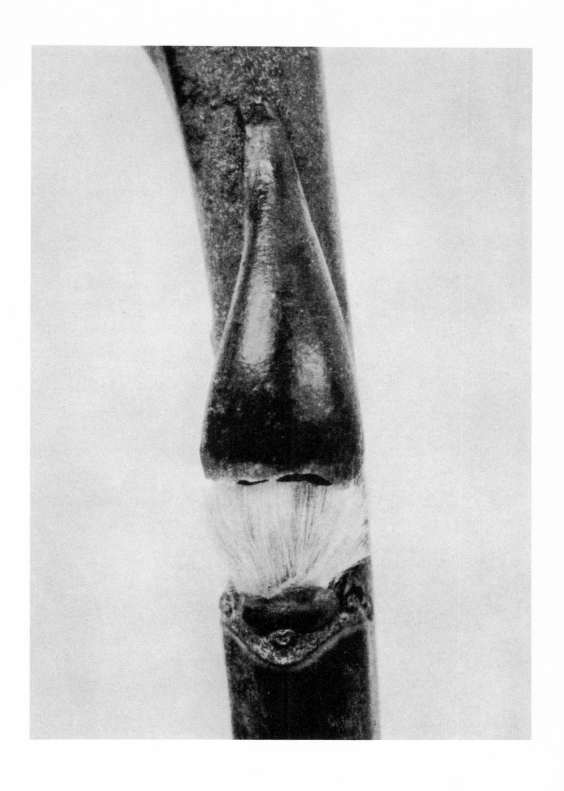

WILLOW

Open Bud
WILLOW
Salix sp. (Tourn.) L.

WILLOW FAMILY   **SALICACEAE**

The plate represents a willow bud which has completed the process of slipping the scale off overhead. Even now the flower-cluster does not stand revealed, for the hairs which tip the inflorescence scales constitute a secondary covering of the young flowers. In a normal expansion of the bud, these hairs stand out evenly all around, and the structure is commonly known as a Willow "pussy." If it were not for these hairs, the stage might be a very critical one, for the protection of the scale has been lost before the flowers are ready for full exposure to drying winds. But the hairs effectively ward off wind and also bright sunlight. Many have imagined the hairy layer to have a temperature modifying influence, but if such exists, it is chiefly a preventive, not a retentive effect; the covering is not a "wool blanket" in the usual sense of the term.

WEEPING WILLOW

Staminate Flower-Clusters
WILLOW
Salix sp. (Tourn.) L.

WILLOW FAMILY   **SALICACEAE**

There are many different forms of Willows, and the various species flower at different periods during the vernal months. Some are very early, while others do not bloom until late. Pollen-bearing and seed-bearing flowers are never carried on the same plant, but both are produced in the same type of elongate inflorescence, or cluster, the catkin.

The Willow pussies so frequently collected in early spring are the immature forms of the catkins. It is the prevailing practice to keep cut willow shoots in containers without water in order to retain the pussies in fuzzy condition, but if the twigs are placed in water immediately after collection, the catkins expand and flowers protrude from their hairy coverlets. In full bloom, staminate catkins are studded with scores of golden pollen masses. Though the flowering stage is short in duration, its surpassing beauty is very alluring, and if one has ever watched willow shoots through their complete flowering, he is never again as desirous to hold them at the pussy stage.

WILLOW

Pistillate Flower
WILLOW
Salix sp. (Tourn.) L.

WILLOW FAMILY   SALICACEAE

Just as the Ginkgo flower represents a
very primitive type among the Gymnosperms, so the Willow exemplifies a simple type among the Angiosperms. The
really distinctive feature of an Angio-
sperm flower is its possession of a pistil, a
structure which encloses the ovules and
persists as a case about the latter when
they have ripened into seeds. From this
point on in the book, flowers which are
seed-bearing only, or buds which contain
such flowers, are referred to by the term
pistillate, just as, from the beginning,
flowers which are stamen-bearing only
have been called staminate.

So simple is the seed-bearing flower of
a Willow that it consists of a single pistil.
This displays typical parts: the case enclosing the ovules, known as the ovary;
the pollen receptive structures at the
apex, called stigmas; and the column
called the style, which joins the ovary
with the stigmas. The whole structure is
connected by its stalk to a scale, which in
turn is attached to the axis of the catkin.

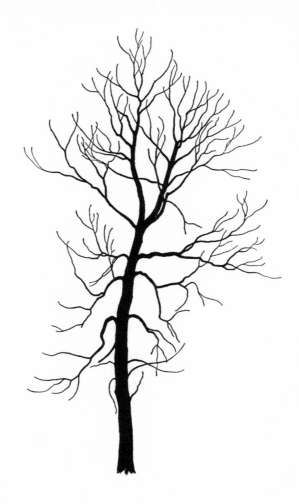

WILLOW

Staminate Flower

WILLOW
Salix sp. (Tourn.) L.

WILLOW FAMILY   SALICACEAE

The staminate flower of the Willow almost matches the pistillate in simplicity.
There are two stamens (more in some
species), each with its anther carried on
the apex of a long stalk, or filament.
These are attached to the same sort of
scale that carries the pistillate flower. The
hairy fringes of the scales constitute the
fuzz at the pussy stage of the catkin. The
prominent column at the base of the
flower is the nectary.

Though the Willows are said to be
largely wind-pollinated, the catkins of
some species are persistently visited by
bees, and it seems not unlikely that the
extent to which insect pollination takes
place in this group of plants has been
underestimated.

In photographing many of the more
minute flowers it was necessary, for the
sake of steadiness, to impale the objects
on the tip of a slender dissecting needle.
The needle tip appears in this and many
other plates of the book.

POLLARDED WILLOWS

A Fruit
WILLOW
Salix sp. (Tourn.) L.

WILLOW FAMILY   **SALICACEAE**

Some of the Willows are as precocious
in maturing their fruits as they are in
producing their flowers. Before summer
has arrived the fruits have ripened and
discharged their seeds. The Willow fruit,
because of its simplicity, offers a good
illustration for a definition of the term.
Technically, a fruit is a ripened flower
pistil, or seed case. The Willow capsule
shown in the plate is a ripened pistil and
it is a case in which the seeds mature.
As might be expected, the part of the
pistil which undergoes the most expansion as the fruit develops, is the ovary.
The style and stigma may persist as lesser
appendages, or they may become completely obliterated. The Willow fruit,
when ripe, splits into two valves which
turn back at the tips and ultimately expose the seeds. Each seed bears a tuft of
long silky hair which, during dispersal,
greatly facilitates carriage by wind.

QUAKING ASPEN

Staminate Flower-Clusters
QUAKING ASPEN
Populus tremuloides Michx.

WILLOW FAMILY   **SALICACEAE**

The Poplars, of which group the Aspen is a member, are very closely related to the Willows, and bear their flowers in the same type of elongate clusters or catkins. But while the Willow catkins stand out more or less stiffly from the twig, those of the Poplar hang pendulous from their attachments. Just as the Willow, however, presents its most pleasing appearance when in flower, so also the Aspen is most decorative when draped with its adornments of fluttering tassels. These, as flowering occurs, increase in length from day to day; the color also changes, for the gray of the hairy covering which is early visible, gives way to maroon or purple as elongation of the axis exposes the flowers.

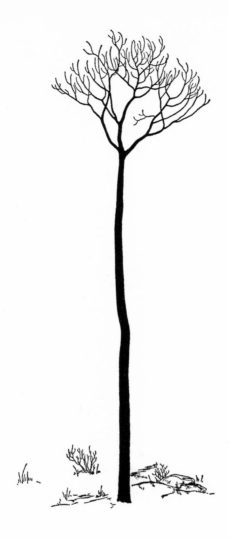

LARGE-TOOTHED ASPEN

Staminate Flower
QUAKING ASPEN
Populus tremuloides Michx.

WILLOW FAMILY   **SALICACEAE**

The flower of the plate was taken from its cluster just prior to the stage of opening of the anthers for pollen release. The several stamens are attached by short stalks to the surface of a disk or shallow cup, and this in turn is attached to the scale. The latter is divided, along its black outer margin, into a series of slender teeth which are fringed with long white hairs. The anthers are red, maroon, or purple.

The progress of blooming of the flowers of a catkin is, in general, from tip to base. In the preceding plate the various phases of blooming are well illustrated. The outermost catkin has completed the discharge of pollen; the intermediate one is mid-way in the process; while the basal one has just begun its elongation, and none of its flowers are farther advanced than the one figured in this plate.

EASTERN COTTONWOOD

[93]

Pistillate Flower
COTTONWOOD
Populus deltoides Marsh.

WILLOW FAMILY   **SALICACEAE**

The staminate catkins of the Cotton-wood are very long, highly colored, flaccid and pendulous; the pistillate clusters are shorter, paler in color, semi-rigid, and hang more stiffly from the twig. Though not conspicuous, they have their own peculiar type of beauty, and this is attributable to the form and rather delicate coloration of the individual flowers and their associated scales.

Each pistil, for the flower consists of a single pistil, is held in a disk or cup, and is comprised of a rounded-conical bright green ovary, surmounted by a crown of whitish stigmas, two to four in number. The variability of lobing and of contour of the stigmas is almost unlimited, and it is largely this feature that makes interesting what might otherwise be a flower without attraction.

These flowers rarely abort, each one maturing into a capsule filled with minute and downy seeds.

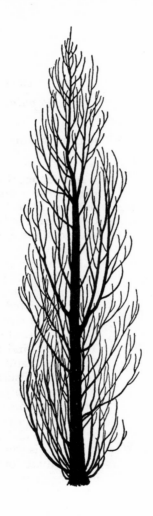

LOMBARDY POPLAR

Fruits
COTTONWOOD
Populus deltoides Marsh.

WILLOW FAMILY **SALICACEAE**

At one time the Cottonwood was widely planted as a street tree. Its popularity suffered a decline, however, when the trees became old enough to bear fruit and scatter their seeds. When large trees loaded with capsules are at dispersal stage, the air in their vicinity is full of flying down. House screens often become so clogged with it that ventilation is seriously interfered with.

The nature of the Poplar fruit is practically identical with that of the Willow. The same kind of silky-haired seeds are developed, and the amount of white down that issues from the capsules of even one inflorescence exceeds the wildest expectation.

Of course the staminate trees do not bear fruits, and do not present the difficulty that is commonly experienced with the pistillate form. The present practice in planting, when Poplars are used, is to favor the staminate trees.

BUTTERNUT

Staminate Flower-Clusters
BUTTERNUT
Juglans cinerea L.

WALNUT FAMILY   **JUGLANDACEAE**

The staminate flowers of the Butternut are borne in catkins which originate from lateral buds near the ends of branches. The embryo catkin issues from the bud in the autumn, but, enlarging only slightly, it remains as a short cone through the winter, its protective covering consisting of the overlapping flower bracts. In spring, after the leaves have expanded somewhat, the catkins begin to elongate and expose their very numerous flowers. Being about the same color as the leaves, the clusters are not at all conspicuous; but an interested seeker need have no difficulty in finding them on the tree, for they are of sufficient size to be easily seen, often reaching a length of several inches. During development, the axis of the cluster is more or less rigid, but at maturity it has attained some degree of flexibility.

BUTTERNUT

Staminate Flower
BUTTERNUT
Juglans cinerea L.

WALNUT FAMILY   JUGLANDACEAE

The staminate catkins of the Butternut bear scores of flowers. These are unusual enough in appearance to warrant a detailed description in order that the plate may be readily understood.

The heavy axis in which the supporting needle is imbedded is the bract which attaches the flower to the axis of the inflorescence. So closely fused with the bract as to be scarcely distinguishable from it, is the calyx, the several lobes of which look like flat fingers grasping the aggregation of stamens. The latter are attached by short filaments to the cup of the calyx and match it closely in color until the pollen ripens, when they become creamy white or yellowish.

With this example of the Butternut, we have reached a point in our series of flowers where a calyx may be expected regularly. The flowers of the Gymnosperms and of the Willow Family were without a calyx, but the Butternut and all the following forms in the book exhibit some type of calyx as a floral feature.

BLACK WALNUT

Pistillate Flower
BLACK WALNUT
Juglans nigra L.

WALNUT FAMILY   JUGLANDACEAE

The seed-bearing flowers of the Black Walnut are borne alone or in clusters of two or three, at the apex of an elongating shoot of the season. Each consists of a flask-shaped pistil, encased in a structure which is generally regarded as consisting of a fusion of the two following elements: first, bracts, or highly modified leaves, which are accessory to but not a true part of the flower itself; and second, a calyx, the four, pointed lobes of which may be seen within the circle of bract tips, and surrounding the bases of the stigmas.

Some authorities state that a corolla exists and that minute petals are inserted in the notches between the calyx lobes. There is not, however, unanimous agreement on this point.

When the fruit matures, the bony nut is surrounded by a fibrous-fleshy husk.

SHAGBARK HICKORY

Staminate Flower
SHAGBARK HICKORY
Carya ovata (Mill.) K. Koch.

WALNUT FAMILY   JUGLANDACEAE

The staminate catkins of the Hickory are peculiar in being forked. The branches are long and the flowers numerous.

Because of the relative absence of fusions it is much easier to understand the parts of this flower and their relations one to the other, than in the case of the pistillate structure of the Hickory. The plate represents a face view of the flower, in contrast with the side view of the staminate flower of the Butternut shown in a preceding plate. The stamens are attached to a calyx, the two blunt lobes of which project on either side above the anthers. The pointed bract, seen protruding between the lobes of the calyx, is attached to that structure only in its basal portion.

After blooming, the flower does not fall from the tree alone; it is the whole staminate catkin that is shed. This seems to be the habit of catkin bearing trees generally.

SHAGBARK HICKORY

Pistillate Flower
SHAGBARK HICKORY
Carya ovata (Mill.) K. Koch.

WALNUT FAMILY   JUGLANDACEAE

This flower is one of several which constitute a cluster at the tip of the new
season's shoot. Through the ground-glass
of the camera it looks like a green urn
with a lobed rim, and piled high with
cracked ice. The flower consists of an ovary surmounted by the watery-translu-
cent stigmas. The structure enclosing the
ovary has, by some, been interpreted as a
calyx with four free lobes. By others, it
is believed to be an involucre composed
of four bracts, or modified leaves, more
or less fused with one another along the
lateral ridges. Whatever the correct inter-
pretation, the structure becomes the husk
of the nut. It differs from the husk of the
Walnut in being hard and in splitting,
when ripe, into four valves, which in this
species of Hickory, fall away freely from
the nut.

IRONWOOD

Pistillate Flowers
IRONWOOD. HOP HORNBEAM
Ostrya virginiana (Mill.) K. Koch.

BIRCH FAMILY   BETULACEAE

The staminate catkins of the Ironwood are typical of the plant family to which the tree belongs. Containing many flowers, they are, when mature, long and pendulous. The seed-bearing catkins, however, are more abbreviated, and are borne somewhat erect, at the ends of short, leafy branches. Each hairy, pointed scale of the cluster carries two flowers, which are tipped by two very long, white stigmas. The ovary of the flower is surrounded by a thin calyx and the whole is enclosed in a hairy sac, or involucre, consisting of fused bracts. While the ovary is maturing into a small nut-like fruit, the enclosing sac increases enormously in size. When full grown at midsummer, the ripened catkin has very much the appearance of the fruit of the Hop-vine, and it is this similarity that is responsible for one of the names which is commonly applied to the tree.

AMERICAN HORNBEAM

Staminate Flower-Cluster
AMERICAN HORNBEAM
Carpinus caroliniana Walt.

BIRCH FAMILY   BETULACEAE

The American Hornbeam, sometimes known as the Blue Beech, is very closely related to the Hop Hornbeam, and resembles it in flower, foliage, and character of the wood, which is exceedingly hard and strong. It differs from its relative in size and in the character of the bark, which fits tightly over the corded surface of the wood, giving the trunk a fluted appearance. The bracts of the fruits, too, instead of being sack-like, are flat, and are strongly lobed along one margin. In autumn they often present a blaze of orange and scarlet, which more than matches the color display of the foliage.

The American Hornbeam produces one of the smallest of staminate catkins. These appear as the leaves are unfolding, and lend a touch of color to the tree in spring, for the outer portions of the scales are bright red.

AMERICAN HORNBEAM

Staminate Flower

AMERICAN HORNBEAM
Carpinus caroliniana Walt.

BIRCH FAMILY   BETULACEAE

This flower has been selected to repre-
sent the pollen-bearers of the Birch Family. Since it differs in some respects from
certain other forms in the family, the
chief points of similarity and of difference will be noted.

All species in the group agree in having the flower associated with a scale of
the catkin. This scale, in the American
Hornbeam, is strongly striped. Both the
Hornbeams develop one flower in connection with each scale, but the Birches
and the Alders may have more than one,
and often have three. The Hornbeams
lack a calyx; the other flowers of the
family possess a calyx. Stamens are numerous in the flowers of Hornbeams,
while few in others. Stamen-filaments are
never much elongated; the protraction
of the common axis of the catkin serving
to expose the anthers almost as effectively as would the lengthening of the individual stalks of the stamens.

[130]

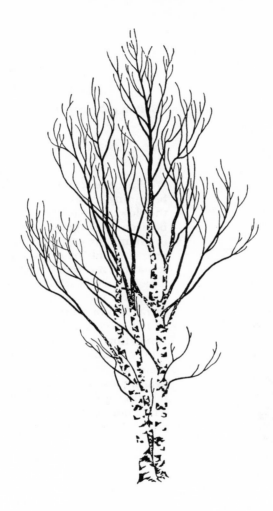

WHITE BIRCH

Flower-Clusters
WHITE BIRCH
Betula alba papyrifera (Marsh.) Spach.

BIRCH FAMILY   BETULACEAE

When the leaves of the Birch are just beginning to take on recognizable form, the flowering catkins of both types may be seen in large numbers on the tree, the staminate in groups of two to several near the ends of twigs, the pistillate terminating the short lateral spur shoots. The stamen-bearing clusters, cylindric, compact, and hard, have been standing through the winter months in a more or less erect position. But now, with the elongation of their axes, they become highly flexible, and droop languidly from their points of attachment. The seed-bearing catkins are short and slender, tapering gradually toward the tip, and while not at all flaccid, they usually lean gracefully away from the perpendicular.

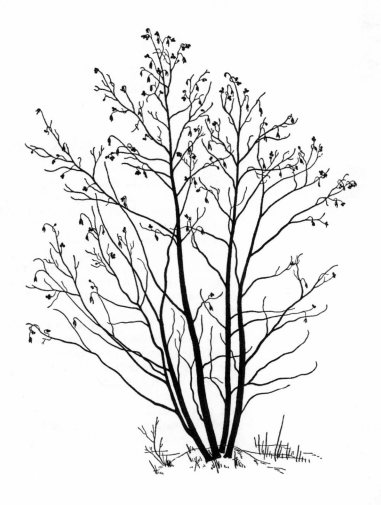

HOARY ALDER

Flower-Clusters
HOARY ALDER
Alnus incana (L.) Moench.

BIRCH FAMILY   BETULACEAE

Among the first flowers to appear in spring are those of the Alders. Even before that first of all vernal herbs, the Skunk Cabbage, is deflorate, the Alder is well on the way to blooming. This is possible because the catkins are formed the previous season, and with the coming of spring, require no further preparation for expansion but only the onset of favorable conditions.

In blooming, the pistillate catkins increase only moderately in size, but the staminate clusters expand to several times their original length. During the period of flowering, the clumps of Alders which may be seen dotting the low grounds, are golden and purple with the pollen-shedding catkins that hang lazily pendant, or stream out in the spring winds.

HOARY ALDER

Staminate Flower

HOARY ALDER

Alnus incana (L.) Moench.

BIRCH FAMILY   **BETULACEAE**

Alder flowers are among the smallest, and would never be seen by anyone but a botanist, were they not massed in catkins. The pistillate clusters contain a score or more of flowers, while the staminate may possess above a hundred. The flowers are attached to, and while forming, are protected by dark purplish red scales which overlap and cover the catkins through the winter. The extension of the catkins at the time of blooming results in radically changing the patterns of form, for the flowers are drawn apart from one another on the axis. Color patterns are also completely altered, for the exposure of new scale surfaces, of stamens, and especially of pollen, results in substituting for the deeper and duller hues of winter the lighter and gayer tints of spring.

Typically there are three staminate flowers to each scale of the catkin. The plate shows a scale with its flowers, one facing to the right, one to the left, and one to the front. Each flower has a four-parted calyx, and each calyx lobe has attached to it a stamen.

BEECH

Flower-Clusters
BEECH
Fagus grandifolia Ehrh.

BEECH FAMILY   **FAGACEAE**

The Beech comes into flower just as the leaves, after having been neatly folded away in winter buds, are spreading out their pleats to the spring sunlight.

The green, pistillate flowers usually occur in pairs on the ends of short, stout stalks, which originate from the axils of upper leaves, and appear to be more or less terminal on the twigs. They are surrounded by numerous hairy bracts, the outer ones being longer than the flowers, and sometimes colored red.

The staminate flowers are aggregated in globular heads, and these are suspended from stalks originating in the axils of lower leaves, or from the shoot below the leaves. Until the individual flowers near maturity, the cluster appears as a hairy, tan-colored ball.

FOREST-GROWN BEECH

Pistillate Flower
BEECH
Fagus grandifolia Ehrh.

BEECH FAMILY   FAGACEAE

Each flower of the pistillate pair, when taken out of its enclosure of bracts, presents a very simple structure. The calyx completely envelops the somewhat three-angled ovary, and is continued upward into four or five hairy, pointed lobes. The three stigmas, corresponding to the cells of the ovary, are rather stout and pointed. They curve outward at the tips, or curl over, forming hooks, or may even coil into miniature croziers.

The smaller bracts about the flower mature into a tough, prickly husk (involucre). This encloses the triangular nuts, which are liberated only after the four valves of the husk have spread apart, about the time of leaf fall in autumn.

From the standpoint of edibility, the Beech nut is regarded by some as having the most delicate flavor of all nuts.

COPPER BEECH

Staminate Flower
BEECH
Fagus grandifolia Ehrh.

BEECH FAMILY   **FAGACEAE**

So completely covered by hairy outgrowths are the young staminate flowers
of Beech that it is not until late in their
development that their real floral nature
becomes evident. It is, however, a very interesting flower to follow through the
process of blooming.

When the flower-clusters first emerge
from their scaly buds, they look like
lumpy masses of light tan-colored hair.
As growth proceeds the lumps become
distinguishable as individual flowers.
The calyx is bell-shaped, the length of
the pointed lobes nearly equalling that
of the tube. Soon the anthers begin to
push out from among the hairs. They
are light olive-green in color and the
combination of this hue with the tan of
the calyx is one of the most unusual to
be seen among tree flowers.

CHESTNUT

Flower-Clusters

CHESTNUT

Castanea dentata (Marsh.) Borkh.

BEECH FAMILY   **FAGACEAE**

The native Chestnut is a disappearing race of trees. Already the Chestnut-Blight disease has killed most of the Chestnut timber of the eastern states, and it is feared that before long the last of it will have vanished before the onslaughts of the destroying fungus.

The Chestnut is a summer flowering form and all other members of its family are well along in fruit formation before it comes into bloom.

The clusters of staminate flowers are very showy, often being half a foot or more in length, and creamy white in color.

Pistillate clusters may be borne in the axils of upper leaves, or sometimes on the basal parts of staminate catkins. Each one is surrounded by an involucre of bright green bracts.

[158]

BLIGHTED CHESTNUT

Pistillate Flowers
CHESTNUT
Castanea dentata (Marsh.) Borkh.

BEECH FAMILY   **FAGACEAE**

    The plate presents a natural cluster of three pistillate flowers from which the surrounding involucre (shown in the preceding plate) has been taken off. Enclosing the pistil of each flower is a hairy calyx with six spreading lobes. Projecting above the calyx are the pure white and rigid styles of the pistil, each one topped by a minute stigma. With the exception of the styles and stigmas, no part of the flower is exposed to the outside world, for the enveloping involucre develops into a bur which remains as a protective structure until the nuts mature. The outer surface of the bur displays a remarkable covering of slender and exceedingly sharp spines, which makes the extraction of the nuts strictly a job for autumn frosts.

BUR OAK

Flower-Clusters
BUR OAK
Quercus macrocarpa Michx.

BEECH FAMILY   FAGACEAE

Most of the Oaks flower late in spring and do not come into bloom until the leaves of the tree have more or less expanded. The pistillate flowers, one or several together, occur in the axils of leaves of the current season. The pollen-bearing flowers are borne in slender, pendulous catkins, which usually originate from lateral buds of the previous season, or from the base of the new season's growth. Both types are present on the branch shown in the plate, the pistillate flower being the small knob in the axil of the leaf third from the tip.

The Oaks are all pollinated by wind, and their flowers may be taken as typical examples of wind pollinated forms, exhibiting such characteristics as large numbers of staminate flowers on wind oscillated axes, lack of nectar, and absence of showiness.

RED OAK

Pistillate Flower
BUR OAK
Quercus macrocarpa **Michx.**

BEECH FAMILY   **FAGACEAE**

The pistillate flower of the Oak is globular in form, and except for the three styles protruding above, is completely enclosed in the hairy scales of the involucre. Inside the latter is a thin calyx which adheres closely to the ovary.

After pollination has occurred, the development of the fruit proceeds rapidly in this Oak and in all others of the White Oak group, so that the acorns are mature at the end of the season. But in the Black or Red Oak group, there is little change in size of the ovary until the beginning of the second season; between the times of pollination of the flower and ripening of the fruit there elapses a period of fifteen or sixteen months.

In some species of Oaks the involucre keeps pace with the growing nut, and at maturity, covers that structure almost as completely as it did the ovary of the flower. In other species, the expanding nut extrudes slowly from the involucre, and the latter finally assumes the form of a shallow cup, or saucer.

WHITE OAK

Staminate Flower
WHITE OAK
Quercus alba L.

BEECH FAMILY   FAGACEAE

The staminate flowers of an Oak out-
number the pistillate, by hundreds to
one. When the catkins issue from the
buds, the flower is compact, and the
membranous calyx tightly clasps the stamens which stand erect on the floral axis.
In spite of the lack of any features of
form which might be regarded as pleasing to the eye, there are, in the flowers
at this stage, pleasing shades of purplish-
brown and yellow that make the clusters
rather attractive objects.

At the time of pollen discharge, the
stamens have elongated, and the anthers
are spread wide apart. The calyx opens
out almost flat. After the pollen is shed,
the dried, brownish remains of the clusters fall from the branch, and all traces
of their presence on the tree are soon
lost.

RED ELM

[177]

Winter Bud
RED ELM. SLIPPERY ELM
Ulmus fulva Michx.

ELM FAMILY   **ULMACEAE**

Tree flowers which are to bloom early in the year must, in the so-called temperate climates, be formed during the preceding growing season. To protect the embryo flowers, laid away in winter buds, various devices are used by woody plants. The most common one is a scaly covering. This is seen in its simplest form in the Willows, where a single scale enwraps the entire bud. The buds of the Elms are covered by a series of scales, laid shingle-fashion about the floral parts, the edges of each scale appressed closely to the one beneath. In the Red Elm, the bud scales are woolly with rusty-red hairs. Such a covering effectively restricts to a minimum the evaporation of water from inner parts. But at the same time it is of such a nature that it can quickly open out to allow the exsertion of structures which must be exposed in order to function.

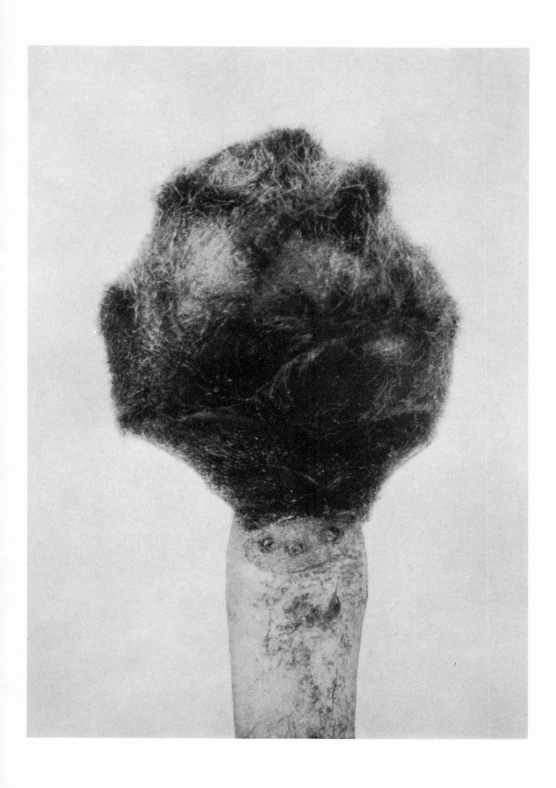

RED ELM

Flower-Clusters
RED ELM. SLIPPERY ELM
Ulmus fulva Michx.

ELM FAMILY   ULMACEAE

The winter buds of the Red Elm are rough, hairy, and rusty-red in color, but their exteriors, while plebeian in appearance, hide structures of surprising beauty. When the bud scales fall away, the compact and radiate clusters stand revealed in all their charm, and the twigs appear as if beset with pompons. The dominant color is light brown, but if a rain falls on the flowers at this stage, all the clusters become tinged with the deep wine-colored pigment of the stamen anthers, and the tree changes greatly in appearance. This phenomenon is possibly unique among our common trees; the writer knows of no other case in which the pigments of a tree flower are water soluble and diffuse out when wetted by rain, coloring other parts to such an extent as to change the color effect of the entire tree crown.

ENGLISH ELM

Flower
RED ELM. SLIPPERY ELM
Ulmus fulva Michx.

ELM FAMILY   ULMACEAE

The flower of the Red Elm is a giant among the flowers of the Elms. No other approaches it in size. It is not at all strikingly colored. The light green of the calyx tube gives way to the bright chestnut of the calyx lobes, and the latter are sparingly fringed with hairs. The stamens are coarse in appearance; the anthers, on thick filaments, are thrust up well above the calyx. The anther walls contain the red or purple pigment referred to on the preceding page. Only the tips of the reddish, hairy stigmas may be seen across the rim of the floral envelope.

Following blooming, the fruit develops rapidly. The ovary wall, enclosing the seed, expands into a broad wing all around. This is the only one of our Elms which has the hairy outgrowths of the fruit confined to the flat face of that organ, and absent from its margins.

AMERICAN ELM

Opening Bud
AMERICAN ELM
Ulmus americana L.

ELM FAMILY   **ULMACEAE**

One of the most interesting features of the tree in winter is the bud. The arrangements, positions, forms, colors, and many other details of bud character differ among the various kinds of woody plants, and serve in winter as distinguishing features of species. But if buds are objects of interest in winter, they are doubly so in spring, for their unfolding reveals ever changing patterns of form, and the successive variety of shades of color displayed is excelled in no other plant part. Perhaps the chief charm of the opening bud lies in this fact that each stage of development is highly ephemeral, and one never finds it looking the same twice in succession.

YOUNG AMERICAN ELM

Opening Flower
AMERICAN ELM
Ulmus americana L.

ELM FAMILY   ULMACEAE

The parts of a flower within the winter bud are arranged very compactly. If a swelling spring bud is opened, one may find the flowers presenting a very different appearance from that exhibited when in full bloom. At first the calyx of the Elm flower completely enwraps the essential parts. But, just as the bud scales are pushed back by expansions from within, so the calyx lobes are forced apart, and the stamens and pistil first see the light of day. The newly exposed surfaces are so fresh as to appear almost moist. The pigments have not been diffused by expansion of the parts containing them; neither have they been subjected to the possibly modifying action of direct sunlight.

Attractive as many tree flowers are when in full bloom, there is something about the earlier stages of development that is never matched later.

CORK ELM

[197]

Flowering Twig
AMERICAN ELM
Ulmus americana L.

ELM FAMILY   ULMACEAE

The American, or White Elm blooms very early in spring, being only a few days later than the Silver Maple, and having a flowering period that coincides approximately with that of the Red Maple.

The clusters of flowers of this Elm are very different in appearance from those of the Red Elm. In the first place, the flowers push out from the ends of the buds, instead of spreading in all directions. This results in carrying the flowers away from the twig, and this effect is accentuated by the considerable lengthening of the flower stalks, or pedicels. Moreover, the degree of lengthening differs among the flowers of a cluster, and the total result is, instead of an even-rayed and perfectly radiate group, as in the Red Elm, a loose and uneven spray.

AMERICAN ELM

Mature Flower
AMERICAN ELM
Ulmus americana L.

ELM FAMILY   ULMACEAE

The typical flower of the Elm is decidedly oblique, but this lack of symmetry
seems to lend added grace to the structure, instead of detracting from it. The
green of the cup of the calyx gives way to
reddish-purple in the lobes. Stamen filaments seem stout for so small a flower.
The anthers, before exsertion from the
calyx, are the richest imaginable blue-
violet in color; later they appear more
red, and finally, after the pollen sacs
open and the creamy white pollen is exposed, the color is purplish-black. The
curved and pointed styles are green, but
the hairy stigmatic surfaces, which cover
the tips, reduce the intensity of the color
to a faint tint.

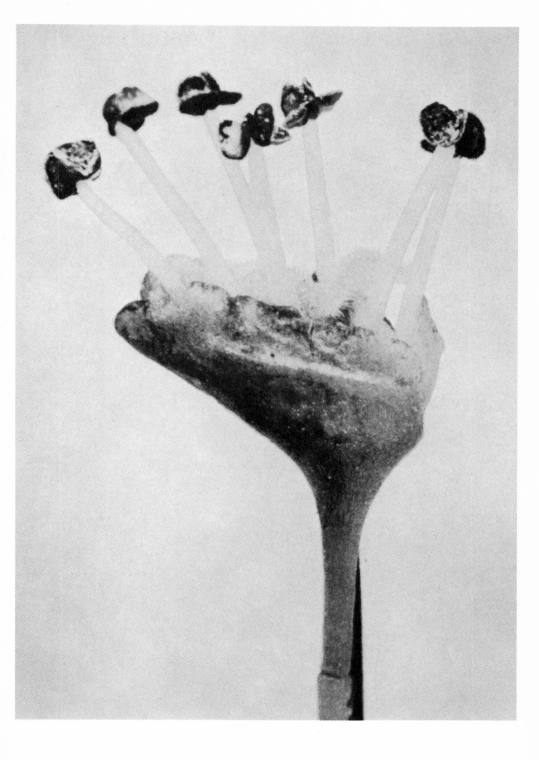

AMERICAN ELM

Developing Fruit
AMERICAN ELM
Ulmus americana L.

ELM FAMILY   ULMACEAE

Among the limited number of forms
which not only flower, but develop their
fruits before the vernal months have
passed, are the Elms. Hardly have the
anthers shed their pollen, before the
pistil, which heretofore has been almost
hidden in the center of the flower,
abruptly enters on a course of rapid expansion. Within a few days the outer
floral parts, which often remain intact,
begin to be dwarfed by the enlarging
pistil. Soon the calyx and the stamen
cycle appear as mere appendages, attached to what now seems, by compari-
son, a giant structure. The color effect
also has changed, for the bright hues of
the calyx have faded, leaving only brown;
the empty anthers are black, but the light
green of the fruit now dominates all, and
does not pale until the time nears for
dispersal.

YOUNG AMERICAN ELM

Fruit
AMERICAN ELM
Ulmus americana L.

ELM FAMILY   **ULMACEAE**

To most people the term "fruit" usually connotes edibility. To the plant,
however, the fruit is an enclosing vessel
for the seed, protecting and nourishing
it up to the stage of maturity. It very
often performs a further office in aiding
in the dispersal of the seed into territory
remote from the parent plant.

Elm seeds are dispersed by wind and
their carriage is greatly facilitated by the
presence of the fruit wall which encloses
the seed. This wall is expanded into a
broad, thin wing about the margin, and
thus, without increasing appreciably the
weight of the body, its carrying possibili-
ties are multiplied by increasing its wind
resistance.

One other feature of this fruit will
bear mention; the small cup at the base
is the old calyx of the flower, which still
adheres even in dispersal.

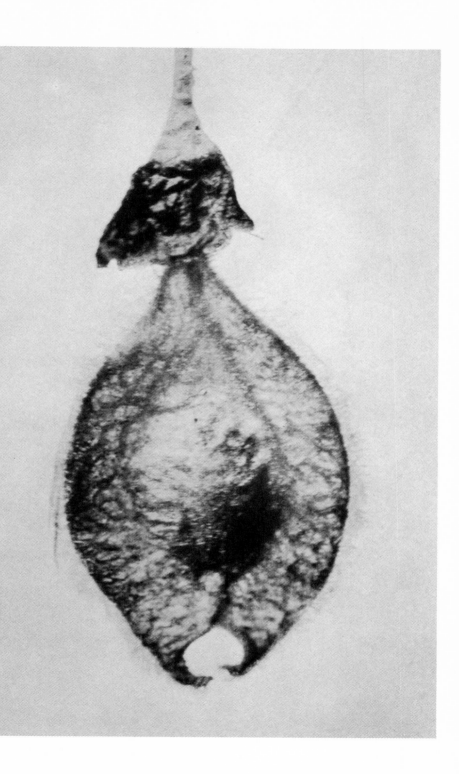

OSAGE ORANGE

Pistillate Flower-Cluster
OSAGE ORANGE
Maclura pomifera (Raf.) Schneider

MULBERRY FAMILY   MORACEAE

The Osage Orange, which produces the famous bow wood of the Osage Indians, occupied in its native habitat in Arkansas, Oklahoma, and Texas, one of the most restricted ranges of any native American tree. But man has carried it far and wide and has planted it in numbers of millions on the treeless areas of the Mississippi basin.

It flowers in early summer. The two kinds of inflorescences appear on different plants. The pistillate clusters are suspended from stalks in the axils of leaves on the thorny shoots of the season. They may be as large as an inch in diameter, and their size is apparently increased by the presence of long white styles of the flowers, which sometimes cover the inflorescence so completely that it could easily pass for a ball of cocoanut shreds. The styles are shed following fertilization, but the remainder of the flower persists into fruit, the compound structures often reaching a diameter of four or five inches.

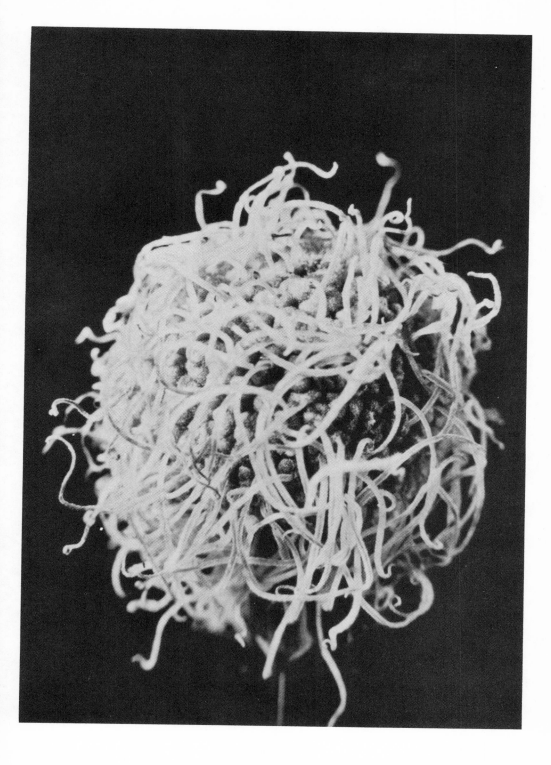

HACKBERRY

Pistillate Flower

OSAGE ORANGE

Maclura pomifera (Raf.) Schneider

MULBERRY FAMILY   MORACEAE

The two kinds of flowers of the Osage Orange are apparently totally unlike, and yet they have the same fundamental plan of structure. The calyx is four lobed. In the staminate flower, the lobes are broadly triangular, thin, and spread wide apart, allowing the free exposure of the four stamens. In the pistillate flower, the lobes are elongated, rather fleshy, and rounded at the ends. Their edges are closely appressed, with the result that the ovary of the pistil is tightly enclosed. The long filiform style protrudes from between the tips of the calyx lobes and the whole structure presents the profile of a narrow grain of corn with its attached silk.

The compound fruit is comprised of scores of the ripened flowers, the calyxes entering into the composition of the structure in the same fashion that they do in the case of the Mulberry. The juice of this fruit is milky and sticky, however, instead of red and watery, as in the Mulberry.

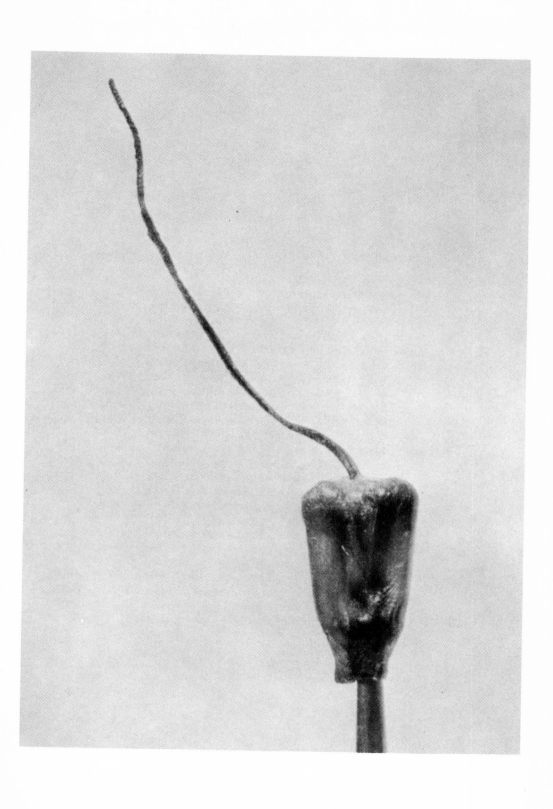

RED MULBERRY

Pistillate Flower-Cluster
RED MULBERRY
Morus rubra L.

MULBERRY FAMILY MORACEAE

About the time that the leaves of the Mulberry are full grown, the compact flower-clusters appear, attached by short stalks near the base of the season's growth, or in the axils of lower leaves.

The pistillate flowers, about a score to a cluster, are as green as the foliage. In each, the ovary is closely surrounded by four thickened sepals, from between the tips of which protrudes the style. This is divided down the middle and because of the hairy stigmatic surfaces, appears almost white.

A peculiarity of this flower is that it becomes, in ripening, a segment of a compound fruit. The entire cluster, or inflorescence, enters into the composition of the fruit; the parts of the calyx appear more or less fused with one another and with the ovary. The whole thing becomes colored and juicy. The Mulberry is almost unique in this respect, inasmuch as only a few other trees produce a fruit of this general character.

CUCUMBER TREE

[225]

Flower

CUCUMBER TREE. MOUNTAIN MAGNOLIA

Magnolia acuminata L.

MAGNOLIA FAMILY   **MAGNOLIACEAE**

The Magnolias stand perhaps first in prominence among our native trees which are known because of their flowers. Not only do these trees have flowers, but everyone recognizes them as such.

While not the showiest of the group, the Cucumber Tree presents a handsome appearance when in bloom. At about the time the leaves unfold, its flowers emerge from hairy sheaths, which have covered the twig tips through the winter, and which usually fall as soon as they have opened. The three short and spreading sepals are green; above them tower the erect greenish-yellow petals, arranged in an outer and an inner series of three each. The petals have a length of as much as three inches and are strongly concave, both longitudinally and across. The stamens are very numerous and are arranged in ranks about the base of the central axis, to which are attached the many pistils. Except the latter, all parts of the flower are soon deciduous. The pistils collectively develop into a cone-like aggregate fruit, which in type is like that of the Blackberry, rather than that of the Mulberry.

TULIP TREE

Flower

YELLOW POPLAR. TULIP TREE
Liriodendron Tulipifera L.

MAGNOLIA FAMILY   MAGNOLIACEAE

The Yellow Poplar is as much an aristocrat among the hardwood trees as the White Pine is among the softwoods. Both trees have been authoritatively reported as growing to a maximum height of two hundred feet, and each bears a foliage which, for beauty, is unexcelled in its class.

In the matter of flowers, the Tulip Tree has the advantage, at least from the standpoint of aesthetics for its floral structures are large and elegant.

The general resemblance of the Tulip Tree flower to that of the Cucumber Tree is obvious, but there are also differences which are distinctive. The numbers of parts are the same, but there is not the great disparity in size between the sepals and petals of the Tulip as in the Cucumber. The petals are shorter, broader, and more blunt, more green than yellow, and distinctly marked with orange at the base.

The fruit is a cone-like aggregation of dry, ripened pistils, which are shed individually, often leaving the central axis on the tree until the following season.

[230]

PAWPAW

Flower

PAWPAW

Asimina triloba Dunal.

CUSTARD APPLE FAMILY   ANONACEAE

The Pawpaw is the most northerly representative of a large family of tropical
plants. It occurs in greatest abundance in
the rich wooded lowlands of the Mississippi valley, and, as a member of the flora
of the region, it presents a noticeably
exotic appearance. This is due principally
to the large, membranous leaves, which
may be a foot in length, and half as wide.
But the flowers, also, are unusual in character and seem foreign to their surroundings. They occur on short, drooping
pedicels in the axils of last year's leaves,
and attain a diameter of one to two
inches. At first, both sepals and the much
larger petals are green, but the latter soon
become brownish and finally a deep wine-
red. There are numerous stamens, and
the pistils are always several or more.
Finally, it might be said that the character of the fruit is in keeping with the
other parts mentioned. It is short, cylindrical, with rounded ends, and soft-fleshy
at maturity, but with seeds so large that
the pulp is scanty. The flavor of the ripe
fruit is so unusual that there is nothing
else with which it can be compared.

[234]

SASSAFRAS

Staminate Flower
SASSAFRAS
Sassafras variifolium (Salisb.) Ktze.

LAUREL FAMILY   LAURACEAE

The Sassafras is, like the Pawpaw, a
member of a tropical group of plants, but
unlike that species it is not the only member of its family to wander far from the
tropics, several other representatives being found in North America.

The flowers appear just before, or with
the leaves, the two kinds being separated
on different trees. They occur at the ends
of twigs, in loose clusters of a few flowers
each. A corolla is lacking, but the pale
yellowish-green calyx has its six sepals
arranged in two series, and the presence
of petals is at least simulated. Another
unusual feature of this flower is the number of stamens, there being normally
nine, arranged in three series. Each
stamen has at its base a pair of orange-
colored glands. But the most interesting
feature of the flower of the Sassafras is the
possession by each stamen anther, of four
valves or lids, which lift, as if hinged, to
allow the discharge of pollen.

WITCH-HAZEL

Flower-Clusters
WITCH-HAZEL
Hamamelis virginiana L.

WITCH-HAZEL FAMILY   HAMAMELIDACEAE

Ordinarily a shrub, the Witch-hazel sometimes reaches the dimensions of a small tree. It is the last of all woody plants to reach the flowering stage each year. So tardily does this occur that in the northern states the flowers are usually full blown only after frosts have terminated the activities of most plants. At a time when the rest of the woodland is in winter condition, with fruits dispersed and leaves amputated, it is startling to find a tree which appears to have just reached its peak of activity. But the Witch-hazel is in no need of a special place in the year; it could command attention at any season, for its flower is one of the most distinctive. Four curved, strap-shaped petals of purest yellow stand out stiffly from the calyx cup, in the bottom of which the stamens form a cross. The pistil, almost unobservable without dissection, is fused with the calyx and the whole structure ripens finally into a woody fruit, which at maturity ejects its two glossy black seeds with great force, hurling them to distances of many feet from the parent plant.

[242]

SWEET GUM

Flower-Clusters
SWEET GUM
Liquidamber Styraciflua L.

WITCH-HAZEL FAMILY   HAMAMELIDACEAE

Few trees seem to be able to produce a gorgeous showing of both flowers and autumnal foliage, and the Sweet Gum is no exception to the general rule. Its floral display is as subdued in green as its autumn foliage is brilliant in red. Nevertheless the flower-clusters do present attractive features of form. Appearing at the tips of upturned twigs all over the tree, they contribute to an effect that is attained for only a brief period, and is peculiarly appealing, partly because of its transitory nature.

The staminate clusters are terminal; each flower appears as a short-stalked, globular mass of stamens without calyx or corolla, but enclosed while young, by four bracts of the involucre.

The flowers of the pendulous, pistillate clusters are compacted into a globular head, and it is only by careful dissection that one can make out the elongated calyx adherent to the ovary, and the minute, abortive stamens attached to the calyx rim. The recurved styles are, of course, obvious, since they practically cover the outer surface of the cluster.

The compound fruit is, in type, like that of the Mulberry and the Osage Orange, but is not juicy.

SYCAMORE

Staminate Flower-Cluster

BUTTONWOOD. SYCAMORE.
PLANE-TREE

Platanus occidentalis L.

PLANE-TREE FAMILY   PLATANACEAE

While the two types of flowers of the
Sycamore occur on the same plant, they
are in different heads, and almost invariably on different stalks. They appear as
the leaves unfold and neither cluster is
conspicuous at the time of flowering.
Both are spherical in form, the staminate
being less than half an inch in diameter,
and the pistillate somewhat larger. So
compact are the clusters that it is only by
dissection that one can get, at first hand,
any adequate idea of the flower. The
plate represents the cut face of a staminate cluster that has been halved. The
calyx and corolla are both present, but
minute, and each consists of three to six
scale-like segments. Opposite each sepal
stands a stamen, with short filament and
a long, two-celled anther, the whole structure capped by a broad plate on the end.

In the seed-bearing flower, the stamens
as well as the sepals and petals are reduced in size and a number of pistils with
long styles make up the bulk of the
flower.

The balls, or "buttons" of the Sycamore
are compound fruits, consisting of many
matured pistils, each with a fringe of
brown hairs, and ultimately separating
from one another in dispersal.

[250]

CRAB APPLE

Flower-Cluster
CRAB APPLE
Pyrus ioensis (Wood) Bailey.

ROSE FAMILY   ROSACEAE

Anyone who, during a woodland ramble, halts in a thicket of wild crab in full flower, has an experience not soon to be forgotten. There is no spring odor superior to that which hovers about a blooming Crab tree. And it is the belief of many that the appearance of the flower is in keeping with its reputation for odor.

The calyx is white-hairy, with lobes widely spreading as the flowers open. The soft-textured petals are usually pink, but sometimes white or rose color. Stamens may be as many as twenty, their filaments diverging widely in direction. The styles, usually five in number, are borne on an ovary which is closely invested by the calyx.

The development of the fruit results more from the thickening of the calyx tube and the tip of the supporting axis, than from the maturing of the ovary wall. The latter is represented in the fruit only by the thin and tough husks which lie immediately about the seeds.

SHAD BUSH

Flower

SHAD BUSH. JUNEBERRY. SERVICEBERRY

Amelanchier canadensis (L.)

ROSE FAMILY   ROSACEAE

The Shad Bush is the earliest tree of its family to flower; even before the woodland is in full leaf the tree is a mass of white bloom. On dry slopes which are almost destitute of other signs of spring, the Shad Bush in flower is especially conspicuous.

The open inflorescences are terminal on new shoots. The white flowers are easily distinguished from those of the Apple, Cherry, or Hawthorn by the fact that the petals are long and narrow.

In the case of the flower shown in the plate, the tips of the petals are pointed, but this condition cannot be said to be altogether typical, for often they are quite blunt. The author sought in vain for a flower exhibiting perfect symmetry; perhaps such are really rare in this species.

There are several other kinds of Shad Bushes; some of them are trees, while others are shrubs. The flowers of the various species differ in minor details, but all of them are readily recognizable as belonging to this group of plants.

[258]

HAWTHORN

Flower-Cluster
HAWTHORN
Crataegus sp. L.

ROSE FAMILY   ROSACEAE

The Crabs, Shad Bushes, and Hawthorns form a more or less natural group
within the Rose Family. In all three the
general characters of the flower-pistil, and
consequently of the fruit, are the same.
But the Hawthorns differ from the other
two in having the mature ovary-walls of
the fruit very hard and bony. They differ
among themselves in many minor details.
For instance, their petals are of various
forms and colors; the number of stamens
in a flower may be five, ten, fifteen,
twenty, or twenty-five, and sometimes intermediate numbers are found. Stamen-
anthers are white, yellow, pink, rose, or
even purple. Styles number from one to
five, in conformity with the number of
compartments in the ovary. Along with
all these differences there is extreme variability, and it is not to be wondered at
that there is no general agreement among
the experts as to how many kinds, or
species, of Hawthorns really exist.

CHOKE CHERRY

Flower-Cluster
CHOKE CHERRY
Prunus virginiana L.

ROSE FAMILY   ROSACEAE

The native trees which belong to the Magnolia Family and to the Rose Family are generally recognized as being flowering plants. In contrast with many other forms, they exhibit floral characters which conform to the commonly held conceptions of what a flower should be. Their flowers are of appreciable size, possess showiness, and bear some resemblance to well-known flowers of the garden or roadside. Any observing and thoughtful person recognizes at once the similarity between the flower of a Wild Rose and that of the Wild Cherry. The similarities are those of form, number of floral cycles, and numbers of parts within the cycles.

The flowers of the Choke Cherry are usually under half an inch in diameter, but they occur in graceful clusters several inches in length, the shorter ones usually erect, the longer ones nodding.

The fruit is rarely edible, its astringent properties not disappearing even after full ripening.

CANADA PLUM

[269]

Flower
CANADA PLUM
Prunus nigra Ait.

ROSE FAMILY   ROSACEAE

About a week or ten days after the Shad Bush has dropped its petals, the Rose Family brings other representatives into prominence in the woodlands, for then the Plums come into flower. Often the crowns of these trees seem to be completely loaded with bloom.

The clusters are few-flowered, and there is no central axis as in the inflorescences of the Choke Cherry and the Shad Bush, but all the flower stalks of a cluster radiate from the same point on the twig. The general color effect of the plant at this stage is pink, for while the petals are normally white, the flower stalks and the calyx are red. However, even the petals may become pink before falling.

The floral characters of the much more widely distributed Wild Plum (*Prunus americana* Marsh.) differ from those of the Canada Plum only in a few minute features.

KENTUCKY COFFEE TREE

Staminate Flower-Cluster

KENTUCKY COFFEE TREE

Gymnocladus dioica (L.) Koch.

LEGUME FAMILY   **LEGUMINOSAE**

The inflorescences of the Kentucky Coffee Tree do not appear until June, and after the tree has been in leaf for some time. The pistillate clusters appear on different trees from the staminate. The latter are the shorter and more compact of the two. Both are produced sparsely on the branches and their delicate tints of green are lost in the midst of foliage which is perhaps the thinnest borne by any of our larger, native trees. Many people who are quite familiar with this tree in the woods have never seen its flowers. Yet it may be found by anyone who searches the tree crown at the proper season. And the finding is reward for the effort. Although the clusters are several inches in length, it is not size that is the striking feature of this inflorescence, but its symmetry, which is as perfect as that of the Hyacinth.

YELLOW WOOD

Staminate Flower
KENTUCKY COFFEE TREE
Gymnocladus dioica (L.) Koch.

LEGUME FAMILY   **LEGUMINOSAE**

So closely associated with our conceptions of the Pea Family is the idea of
bilateral flowers, that a radial flower on a
leguminous plant seems a distinct anom-
aly. But the flower of the Kentucky Coffee
Tree is, in all its visible features, as radi-
ally symmetrical as a buttercup or a rose.
The calyx cup is topped by its five lobes,
which are shorter, narrower, and more
pointed than the petals. The stamens, ten
in number, are erect and are inserted with
the petals on the rim of the calyx cup.
The pistil, in the staminate flower, is
reduced to a mere rudiment, or is lacking altogether.

In general appearance, the pistillate
flower differs little from the staminate,
the pistil being a relatively inconspicuous
feature. Though the flower has a full
complement of stamens, the filaments are
short and the anthers are sterile.

[278]

HONEY LOCUST

Pistillate Flower
HONEY LOCUST
Gleditsia triacanthos L.

LEGUME FAMILY   **LEGUMINOSAE**

From the axils on the previous season's twigs, both flowers of the Honey Locust grow in short and inconspicuous clusters.

Although pistils and stamens are usually borne in different flowers, they occasionally occur together. Pistillate flowers do appear to have stamens, but the structures are present in form only; no pollen is produced, and the parts therefore do not function. An examination of the plate will show that the anthers of the stamens are shriveled and abortive.

The whole flower is greenish in color. The calyx has from three to five lobes (four in the flower photographed) and an equal number of petals. Stamens may vary widely in number. The three sets of parts just named are placed in perfect symmetry about the center; only the goose-neck pistil seems to be out of harmony with this arrangement, and bends off to one side.

The fruit is a flat bean, often a foot or more in length, dark reddish-brown in color, and usually more or less twisted.

[282]

REDBUD

Flower

REDBUD

Cercis canadensis L.

LEGUME FAMILY   **LEGUMINOSAE**

Over a large section of eastern United States, a most impressive occurrence of the vernal season is the flowering of the Redbud. No other of our trees produces a flower of anything like its color, and when in bloom, few indeed exceed it for conspicuousness on the landscape. The flowering period often precedes the unfolding of the leaves; twigs and larger branches appear crowded with the rose-purple blooms, and flower clusters may sometimes be seen even on the trunks of the trees. Though not an extreme expression of the legume type, the individual flower exhibits strongly the two-sided form or bilateral symmetry that so widely characterizes the family to which it belongs. The calyx, which is cup-like, is the more deeply colored part; it is a rich purple, while the corolla is rose-color. The stamens and the pistil are enclosed and hidden by the lower petals. By midsummer, the pistil has developed into a flat legume, of much the same color as the petals of the flower, but later turning brown. It remains on the tree until fall or early winter.

COMMON LOCUST

Flower-Cluster
COMMON LOCUST. BLACK LOCUST
Robinia Pseudo-Acacia L.

LEGUME FAMILY   LEGUMINOSAE

The Locust is, among our trees, perhaps the most typical representative of the Pea Family, for it bears flowers of the true "butterfly" type. These develop in short clusters on a common axis, from the axils of the compound leaves. The time of flowering is about the first of June, being somewhat earlier in the South, and later northward.

The petals are entirely white, with the exception of the large upper one, or standard, which is yellowish near the base. Not only are the flowers showy, but they possess a fragrance equal in quality to their appearance, and rivalling that of the Sweet Pea.

The legume, or "pod," when mature, is three or four inches long. The dull brown of its exterior is often relieved by the glistening white of the inner surfaces of the two valves, which tend to separate while still attached to the stalk. The fruits may be still hanging on the tree many months after ripening.

STAGHORN SUMAC

Pistillate Flower-Cluster
STAGHORN SUMAC
Rhus typhina L.

SUMACH FAMILY   ANACARDIACEAE

With most people all the Sumachs have a bad reputation, just because one of them is an exceedingly dangerous plant. Very few people, however, have occasion to be alarmed about the possibility of Sumach poisoning, for, with the exception of hunters, woodchoppers, and a few venturesome vacationists, practically no one ever sees a plant of the poisonous species. It inhabits low swamps exclusively. In the details of appearance of leaf, twig, flower-cluster, and fruit, it is quite different from the common varieties of Sumach.

The flower-clusters of the Staghorn Sumach appear in early or mid-summer, at the tips of the stout branches. Their greenish white color leaves them decidedly lacking in conspicuousness, and it is only when they project above the crown of the foliage that they are apt to attract the eye. They do, however, present a pleasing appearance against their background of darker foliage.

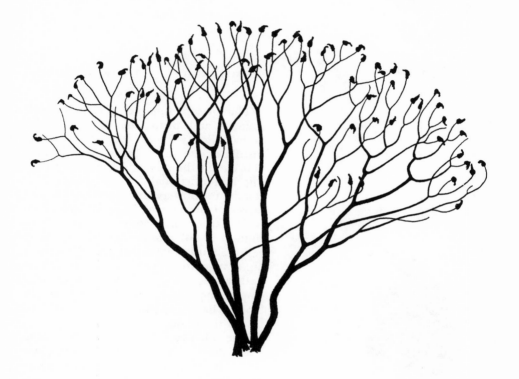

STAGHORN SUMAC

✱

Staminate Flower
STAGHORN SUMAC
Rhus typhina L.

SUMACH FAMILY   **ANACARDIACEAE**

Though sometimes complete, with both
stamens and pistil, the flowers of the
Sumach are typically either staminate or
pistillate, the pistil being reduced and
abortive in the one, and the stamens being non-functional in the other. The
staminate clusters are considerably the
larger of the two, and usually are somewhat earlier in blooming. They differ
slightly in color too, being more nearly
yellow, with stamen anthers displaying
an orange hue. The staminate flowers
wither after blooming, and finally fall,
leaving the branched stalks of the clusters
looking bare, and inharmonious with the
rest of the plant.

The pistillate flowers on the other
hand, develop into handsome fruits, the
narrowly pyramidal clusters of which display their brilliant crimson from late
summer into the winter months. They
are at their maximum of attractiveness,
however, only a few weeks after the flowering stage. At that time the hairy surfaces of the ovaries have only in part
taken on their red tints, and the contrast
with the rich greens of the less advanced
surfaces is very striking.

HOLLY

Pistillate Flower
HOLLY
Ilex opaca Ait.

HOLLY FAMILY   AQUIFOLIACEAE

Few people are unfamiliar with the fruiting branches of Holly so widely displayed and sold at the Christmas season. But, at least in the northern states, not many are familiar with the flower from which the brilliant red berry develops. Probably still fewer know that many Holly trees do not bear fruits at all; these are plants the flowers of which are exclusively staminate.

The staminate and pistillate flowers are much alike in general appearance but of course they differ in detail. The former occur in clusters of several, on shoots of the season, but drop off soon after the opening of the anthers. The pistillate flower is more often solitary on a short stalk, near the base of the season's shoot, or in the axil of a leaf. Its calyx-lobes, petals, and sterile stamens are in fours. The pistil is bright green, short and columnar, with a broad stigmatic cap resting on the ovary. The berry does not ripen until late autumn, but it remains on the branch through the winter. The use of Holly for holiday decorations has brought about serious inroads on the supply, and the tree in some localities is in danger of extermination.

WAAHOO

Flower

BURNING BUSH. WAAHOO

Evonymus atropurpureus Jacq.

STAFF TREE FAMILY   CELASTRACEAE

The Burning Bush is sometimes classed as a shrub, but it often displays tree form and usually attains the height of a small tree.

The flowers are displayed at the tips of trichotomously branched stalks, which originate in the axils of leaves or from near the base of the season's growth. The central feature of the flower is the expanded end (disk) of the floral axis, which covers the ovary completely, allowing only the exposure of the stigma. On the disk, near each of the four corners, is a stamen anther, apparently sessile and producing cream-colored pollen. Both the disk and the petals are deep maroon and their surfaces are velvety in appearance. The four minute lobes of the calyx are visible at the angles between the petals.

The fruit is as distinctive in appearance as the flower. Its four lobes are light purple in color. Each splits below to expose a seed, which is covered by a thin, scarlet coat. A Waahoo tree in full fruit is fully as showy as the Winterberry in like stage.

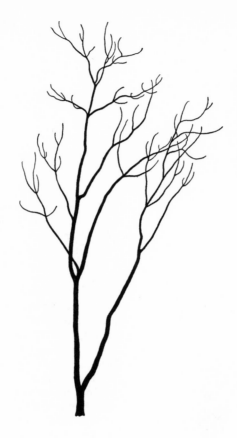

BLADDERNUT

Flower-Clusters

BLADDERNUT

Staphylea trifolia L.

BLADDERNUT FAMILY   **STAPHYLEACEAE**

The Bladdernut is strictly a shrub in habit, but sometimes attains the height of a small tree. It is the only representative of its family in eastern United States, though there is another in California.

The branched and drooping flower-clusters appear in mid-spring, from the axils of the three parted foliage leaves. The flowers are cylindrical bell-shaped. The five sepals are very similar to the petals, but are slightly shorter and without spreading tips. Both sepals and petals are pure white in color, or the sepals may have a tinge of green. Equalling the petals in number and length are the stamens, which open their yellow anthers at the mouth of the flower. The ovary is three-parted at its summit, but the styles cohere sufficiently to appear as one.

When ripe, the fruit is a greatly inflated capsule, three lobed, with tough, papery walls, and turning reddish-brown late in the autumn. It may be found hanging on the branches long after the compound leaves have been shed.

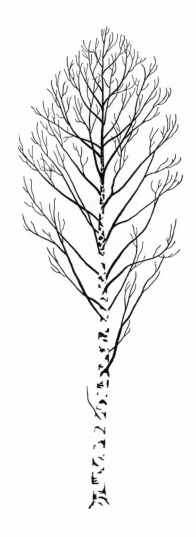

WHITE BIRCH

RED MAPLE

Acer rubrum L.

MAPLE FAMILY   **ACERACEAE**

Almost none of our woody plants is without externally visible buds throughout the winter season. Yet most people think that buds are first formed in the spring. An examination of a winter twig of the nearest tree would serve to dispel that notion from any mind that harbors it. The arrangements, positions, forms, colors, and many other details of bud character differ among the various kinds of plants, and serve in winter as distinguishing features of the species just as differences of flower and leaf do in summer. It is just this variety of characteristics that proves surprising to those who have always considered the book of nature as more than half closed in winter, and who, when they look for items of interest, find in the winter condition of plants a matter of great fascination. While buds of the so-called naked types are without any special coverings, except perhaps hairy outgrowths, the majority of buds are encased in scales. Bud scales are, in reality, leaves which have been modified in the course of time to serve a protective instead of a nutritive function.

RED MAPLE

Opening Winter Bud
RED MAPLE
Acer rubrum L.

MAPLE FAMILY   ACERACEAE

Progress in the spring opening of winter buds may be rapid or slow, continuous or intermittent. The rate at which the various stages succeed one another shows the closest dependence on the weather. If the air becomes chilled, buds may remain for days in whatever phase the lowered temperature finds them. But if sunshine permeates all out-of-doors, bringing that stimulating warmth that seems peculiar to spring alone, buds develop with a speed that carries them through to completion in an incredibly brief space of time. When the scales have spread sufficiently, the dark ruby tips of the young flowers begin to appear. With the elongation of their individual stalks, the flowers are pushed upward, and by the time for their opening, have been elevated to the level of the top of the bud. At this stage, the contrast between the intensely dark red of the floral parts, and the soft, light brownish tints of the inner scale surfaces is very striking indeed.

STRIPED MAPLE. MOOSEWOOD

Open Bud with Staminate Flowers
RED MAPLE
Acer rubrum L.

MAPLE FAMILY   **ACERACEAE**

Bud scales are remarkably efficient as protective structures, but they have a limited period of usefulness. When the time comes for the functioning of parts which they enclose, the scales are forced apart by growth expansions and are ultimately discarded altogether.

The opening or unfolding of the bud is an event of considerable interest. Among buds easily obtained for observation are those of the Soft Maples, trees which are widely distributed through the low forest lands of eastern United States, and which are widely planted as shade trees in town and city streets. Their buds develop early; hardly is the frost out of the ground before a decided enlargement may be noticed. Then, as expansion continues, new scale surfaces which were previously hidden by overlapping, become more and more exposed, and the tints displayed at this stage rival those which are exhibited after the flowers open.

SILVER MAPLE

Mature Staminate Buds
SILVER MAPLE
Acer saccharinum L.

MAPLE FAMILY   ACERACEAE

Buds which are borne laterally on twigs are ordinarily produced in the axils of leaves, and after leaf-fall they appear just above the leaf scars. In the Maple Family there are two leaves opposite one another at each node or joint on the twig, and the axillary buds are therefore also opposite. But the Maples characteristically produce other buds which stand alongside those in the axils, and thus a node of the stem often carries as many as five buds, all of which may produce flowers in season.

When one steps out under the street Maples on an early spring day, he may know without looking up that the trees are in full flower, for the drone of hundreds of bees is evidence that nectar and pollen are being exposed. A staminate Red or Silver Maple in full bloom under the spring sun is a blaze of gold and red.

YOUNG SWEET GUM

Very Young Staminate Flower
RED MAPLE
Acer rubrum L.

MAPLE FAMILY   ACERACEAE

If, before growth starts in the spring, a winter bud is opened, one may find flowers there in a surprisingly advanced state of development. All the parts which appear later are present but of course in an unexpanded condition. It need not astonish anyone, therefore, that flower growth proceeds with such rapidity; the only necessity is for the plant to spread the already formed substances on a large volume of absorbed water.

The plate shows a staminate flower that was taken out of a bud which had not yet opened. The calyx and the stamen anthers stand out prominently; the petals may be seen in the notches between the calyx lobes. At this stage, the base of the calyx is greenish, but it shades into yellow in the tube; the tips of the lobes and of the petals are reddish. The anthers are blood red.

YOUNG TREE OF HEAVEN

Young Staminate Flower
RED MAPLE
Acer rubrum L.

MAPLE FAMILY   ACERACEAE

The development stage represented in the plate is approximately the time of appearance of the anther tips between the scales of the opening bud. The stalk has elongated, and the sepals and petals have enlarged considerably. Already the green of the floral envelopes has been almost completely replaced by golden yellow, except where the red of the sepal and petal tips is being intensified. The deep blood red of the anthers remains almost unchanged, while the color seems to accentuate the pebbling of the surface. Each individual marking represents the extent of one of the cells which make up the anther wall. The stamen filaments have only started to lengthen.

BOX ELDER

Open Staminate Flower
SILVER MAPLE
Acer saccharinum L.

MAPLE FAMILY   ACERACEAE

While the bud as a whole is unfolding,
the flowers within are pursuing a parallel
course. Soon the stage is reached at which
the stamen filaments elongate and the
calyx lobes spread. The number of these
lobes varies in different flowers, but is
usually five or six. Mentioned before are
the absence of the corolla, and the fact
that this is one of the characters which
helps to distinguish the Silver Maple
from its very similar and close relative
the Red Maple. The calyx, however, is
colored like a corolla, and passes for one,
with most observers. A pistil is either entirely lacking, or consists of a minute
rudiment, barely discernible at the center
of the flower.

YOUNG SILVER MAPLE

Mature Staminate Flower
SILVER MAPLE
Acer saccharinum L.

MAPLE FAMILY   **ACERACEAE**

The flower of the plate was taken from a fully expanded bud, like that of Plate 327, and represents the grand climax of development in the staminate series. All parts have attained their maximum size. The stamen filaments now look like long, slender threads of ice. The anther sacs have split longitudinally, exposing the yellow pollen masses which show with great distinctness against the now purplish-black anther walls. Usually about five or six of these flowers are produced in one bud. After the flower blooms, the stamens are the first of the parts to wilt; then the calyx shrivels. Finally, after a lapse of perhaps days, the whole bud drops from the twig and all traces of pollen-bearing flowers are lost from the tree.

STREET MAPLE

Pistillate Bud

RED MAPLE

Acer rubrum L.

MAPLE FAMILY   ACERACEAE

The Maple Family contains species which sometimes produce stamens and pistil in the same flower; it includes other species which sometimes develop staminate and pistillate flowers in the same cluster. But the common Soft Maples, the Red and the Silver, have the two kinds of flowers separate, and in different clusters, though they may be on the same tree.

Several stages in the development of buds containing staminate flowers have been portrayed on preceding pages. This plate represents an early stage in the opening of a bud which contains pistillate flowers. The bud has swollen to the point of opening and the tips of the bright red styles are showing through between the scales.

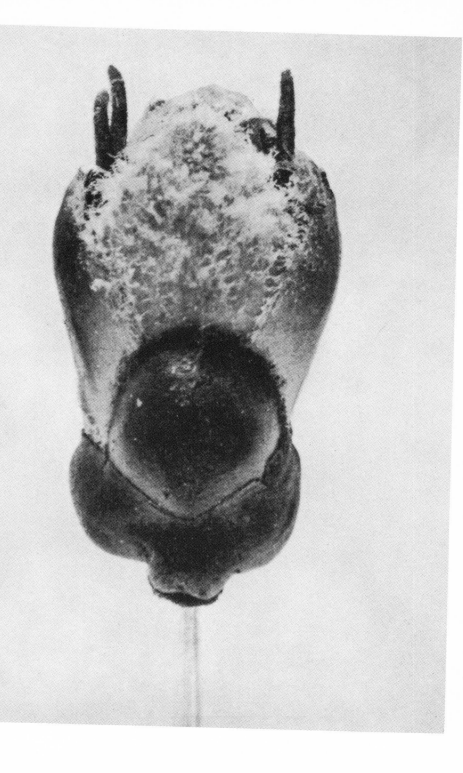

STREET MAPLE

Open Pistillate Bud
RED MAPLE
Acer rubrum L.

MAPLE FAMILY   **ACERACEAE**

While the name of the Red Maple was undoubtedly applied to the tree because of the color of its autumn foliage, the appellation could just as appropriately have been assigned because of the appearance of the pistillate trees during the period of flowering. From the time the buds begin to open until long after the stage of pollination of the flowers, the dominant color throughout the crown of the tree is deep red. Though the bud as a whole shows striking symmetry at almost any stage of development, even up to maturity of its flowers, its most impressive feature is the intensity of its ascendant color.

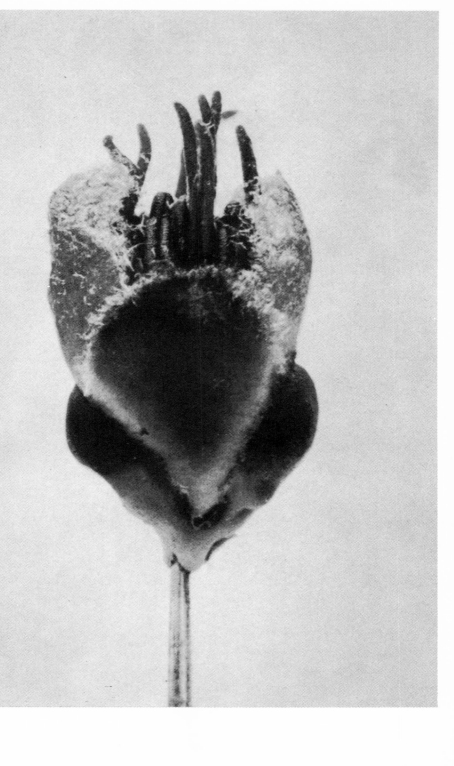

STREET MAPLE

Maturing Pistillate Bud
RED MAPLE
Acer rubrum L.

Seemingly reluctant to give up the protectorate over their enclosed flowers, the scales of the bud open only far enough to allow the crowded exit of the floral structures. As the flowers emerge, two prominent features of the Red Maple, which do not occur in the Silver Maple, are brought into evidence. One, the possession of petals, has been mentioned previously. The other is the great lengthening of the flower stalks, or pedicels, which in their growth, carry the flower well outside of the enclosure of the bud scales. Each pistillate bud produces four or five flowers, and when four to six buds open at one node on the stem, the mass of bloom is considerable.

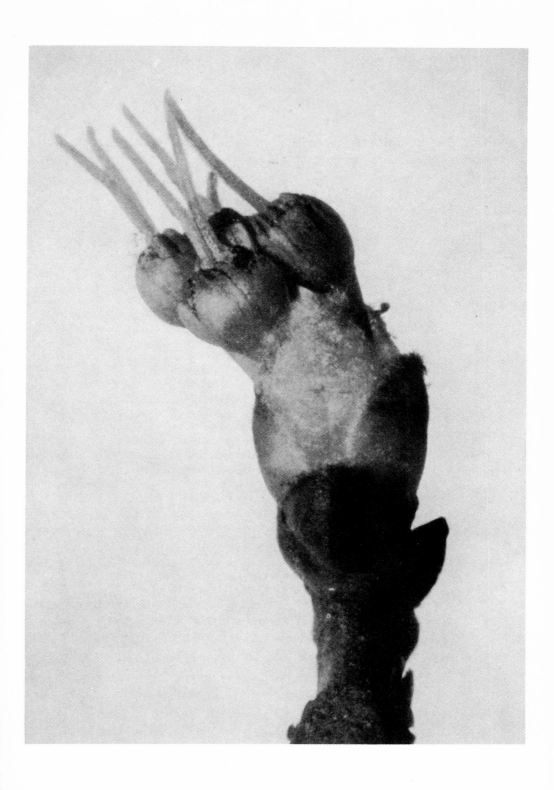

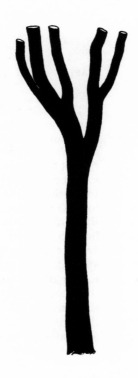

STREET MAPLE

Mature Pistillate Bud
RED MAPLE
Acer rubrum L.

MAPLE FAMILY   ACERACEAE

The plate shows a cluster of pistillate flowers at their peak of development. It is the time of transfer of pollen from the anthers of staminate flowers to the stigmas of these, and anything which follows may be referred to as a phase of fruit formation. At full bloom, the bases of the long flower pedicels are still held in the dark urn of the bud scales. The latter have played an important, even though an accessory part in development, but in spite of the fact that they are now no longer of any practical use to the plant, they persist long after flowering. Indeed they are so tough and so well attached that the fruits may have reached maturity and fallen before the scales weather off from the plant.

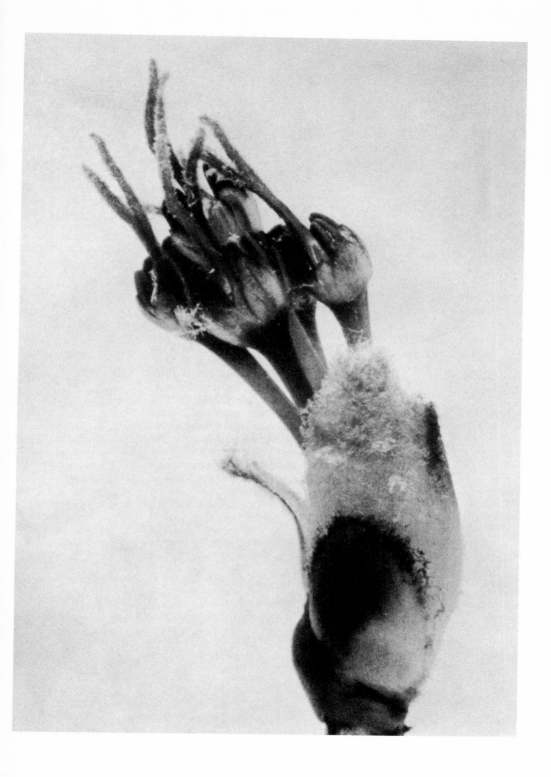

YOUNG SILVER MAPLE

Young Pistillate Flower
RED MAPLE
Acer rubrum L.

MAPLE FAMILY   ACERACEAE

It is difficult for even an experienced student of plant life to avoid surprise when, on opening a bud in midwinter, he finds therein flowers which, to all appearances, are capable of expanding into bloom the following day. Yet nothing can be more obvious than the fact that the floral structures which appear with such suddenness on one of the first spring days must have had a long period of prior development, else they could not appear ready-made at the first onset of favorable temperatures.

The flower of the plate was taken from a bud in earliest spring, and it already possessed the deep red coloration which is so striking a feature of the flower at the time of full bloom.

FOREST-GROWN SILVER MAPLE

Mature Pistillate Flower
SILVER MAPLE
Acer saccharinum L.

MAPLE FAMILY   **ACERACEAE**

To any casual observer, the flower of
the plate would seem to be "perfect" in
the botanical sense of possessing both
pistil and stamens. The presence of the
pistil is evidenced by the two erect and
pointed styles with their rough stigmatic
surfaces. Moreover, the pistil is func-
tional, for flowers of this type produce
fruit and set seed. But the stamens are
present in form only. It is true that the
anthers are plump, and they appear capable of functioning; but if one follows the
flower in its further development, he will
find that the stamen filaments do not
elongate and that the anthers never open
and therefore do not discharge pollen.
No corolla is present. The calyx lobes
vary in number and in form; sometimes
they are reduced to mere irregularities
on the rim of the calyx cup.

CLUMP OF YOUNG SILVER MAPLES

Young Fruit
RED MAPLE
Acer rubrum L.

MAPLE FAMILY   ACERACEAE

The Soft Maples are precocious not only in bearing flowers, but also in producing their fruits. Apparently, fertilization of the ovules follows very soon after pollination. At any rate, it is a matter of only a few days after blooming before the ovule case, or ovary, can be seen to have markedly enlarged. The styles shrivel early, and the two divergent tips of the ovary soon protrude above the calyx. As expansion of the young fruit proceeds, the outer parts of the flower drop away one by one; sepals, petals, and abortive stamens are all ultimately discarded.

The plate illustrates a rather early stage in fruit development; the floral parts, with the exception of the styles, being still intact.

MOUNTAIN MAPLE

Mature Fruits
MOUNTAIN MAPLE
Acer spicatum Lam.

MAPLE FAMILY   **ACERACEAE**

The Red and Silver Maples mature
and disperse their fruits in spring, usually before the leaves are full grown; the
enclosed seeds germinate and seedlings
may be well established in the soil before
the time of frost. But other nearly related
Maples, such as the Sugar Maple, the Ash-
leaved Maple, and the Mountain Maple,
do not ripen their fruits until autumn.

By most people, the fruit of the Maple
is called a seed. But it is more than a seed,
for the outside case of the structure is the
ripened ovary wall of the flower pistil. It
is this part which expands into the broad
wings and facilitates dispersal.

Fruits of the Mountain Maple are unusual among those of the Maple group
in displaying an autumnal coloration
equal or even superior to that of the
foliage of the tree that bears them.

HARD MAPLE

Staminate Flower
HARD MAPLE
Acer saccharum Marsh.

MAPLE FAMILY   **ACERACEAE**

The bell-shaped flowers of this Maple
hang suspended at the ends of thread-like
pedicels, which may have a length of as
much as three inches. The two types of
flowers, pistillate and staminate, may be
borne in the same cluster, or in separate
clusters, and sometimes the two kinds are
on different trees. While the staminate
flower shows little or no trace of a pistil,
the pistillate flower possesses its complement of stamens, usually about eight, but
these do not produce viable pollen. There
is no corolla and the calyx is only shal-
lowly lobed. After blooming, the staminate flowers shrivel and drop from the
twigs, often in their natural clusters. The
pistillate flowers remain on the tree and
slowly develop their winged fruits. These,
in contrast with the fruits of the Silver
and the Red Maples, do not become fully
mature until autumn. Again, in contrast
with the two forms named, the winged
bodies are often shed free from the
pedicels, leaving the latter hanging on
the tree through the following winter.

NORWAY MAPLE

Staminate Flower
NORWAY MAPLE
Acer platanoides L.

MAPLE FAMILY   ACERACEAE

The Norway Maple, while not a native tree, has long been planted in the streets and parks of this country. It is one of the finest of the Maples, possessing a well shaped crown, beautiful foliage, a clean bark of interesting pattern, and exquisite clusters of flowers.

The two types of flower-clusters expand with the leaves and are loose and open. Their color is cream, or light yellow, but there is a tinge of green with it. The individual flowers have a wider spread than those of any native Maple. The sepals and petals are usually five each in number, the latter being somewhat more delicate in form, if not in coloring. Standing up from the surface of the broad disk are the eight stamens. At the center of the flower, a pistil, if represented at all, occurs only as a rudiment.

NORWAY MAPLE

Pistillate Flower
NORWAY MAPLE
Acer platanoides L.

MAPLE FAMILY   ACERACEAE

There is little difference in the appearance of the staminate and pistillate flower-clusters of the Norway Maple. The individual flowers of the two kinds are alike in size, form, and color. The pistillate flower even has the characteristic number of stamens, though the filaments never reach full length, and the anthers do not open; they therefore do not discharge pollen. The distinguishing feature of the flower is, of course, the pistil, which may be seen in its central position, the two edges of the ovary already widely expanded, prophetic of the enormous wings which the fruit is finally to display. The fruit is the most distinctive possessed by any of the Maples, the wings standing out almost at right angles with the central axis.

SYCAMORE MAPLE

Pistillate Flower
SYCAMORE MAPLE
Acer pseudo-platanus L.

MAPLE FAMILY   **ACERACEAE**

Like the Norway Maple, the Sycamore Maple is a native of Europe. While not used in the United States nearly as much as the first-named tree, it does constitute an unusual and interesting form in the plantings of many cities, particularly in the East. Differing in many respects from the Norway Maple, it is no less attractive as a tree, and would be highly prized as an ornamental, except for one feature; it does not seem to thrive as well under our conditions as at home, and many planted trees fail to reach maturity.

The flower clusters are long and slender and not nearly so showy as those of the Norway Maple. The pistillate flower possesses stamens, but they are non-functional. The most distinctive feature of the flower is the hairy ovary of the pistil.

HORSE-CHESTNUT

Flower-Cluster
HORSE-CHESTNUT
Aesculus Hippocastanum L.

BUCKEYE FAMILY   **HIPPOCASTANACEAE**

There are only a few kinds of street trees that are planted with the thought in mind that their flowers will add to the appearance of the street. The Horse-chestnut is undoubtedly the most prominent of the number. Its use is, of course, much more common in Europe than in America. Solotaroff states, in his "Shade Trees in Towns and Cities," that there are seventeen thousand trees of this species in the streets of Paris, and that the flowering of a plantation of Horse-chestnut in a London park is an eagerly anticipated event which brings out the public to view the display.

The flower clusters, sometimes a foot in length, are terminal on upturned branches, and a single tree may have hundreds of these in bloom at one time. The individual flowers are white, with splotches of purple and yellow. They are short lived, and give way soon to the globular, prickly fruits, which contain glossy brown seeds, much prized by small boys as pocket-pieces.

OHIO BUCKEYE

Flower
OHIO BUCKEYE
Aesculus glabra Willd.

BUCKEYE FAMILY   HIPPOCASTANACEAE

The Buckeye is very closely related to the Horse-chestnut, but its flower clusters as well as the individual flowers are smaller and by no means so showy. The color is a light and not very bright yellow.

This flower exhibits a rather unusual feature in having a different number of parts in each cycle. There are five lobes of the calyx, four petals, seven stamens (sometimes one more or less), and one pistil. The flower is strongly two-sided, or bilaterally symmetrical, the petals being arranged in two pairs, a lateral, and an upper. The outer ends of the upper petals are turned abruptly erect, and the inner surfaces are sometimes streaked with red.

The fruits and seeds, like the flowers, are smaller than those of the Horse-chestnut.

[398]

CAROLINA BUCKTHORN

Flower

CAROLINA BUCKTHORN
INDIAN CHERRY
Rhamnus caroliniana Walt.

BUCKTHORN FAMILY   **RHAMNACEAE**

To anyone engaged in a search for decorative forms in floral structures, a view of the Buckthorn flower, together with a realization of its small size, would be sure to bring disappointment. If this flower were larger, its perfect, pleasing symmetry and crisp angularity would make it a favorite form.

The few-flowered clusters are borne in the axils of leaves of the season. The color is white or greenish white. From the well developed cup of the calyx the five calyx-lobes spread almost at right angles to the axis. It is almost impossible to recognize the minute petals, partly because of their size, but also because they enwrap the stamens.

When the fruit is mature, it is a small black berry which persists on the branches for only a limited time.

BASSWOOD COPPICE

Flower-Cluster

BASSWOOD. AMERICAN LINDEN

Tilia americana L.

LINDEN FAMILY   **TILIACEAE**

The Basswood is noted for the beauty of its form, flower, and foliage. Its wood is of the highest usefulness. It is widely utilized as a shade tree, and the nectar that it produces is so favored by bees that the tree is often called Bee Tree. The honey made from the nectar is said to be unexcelled in flavor and delicacy.

By midsummer, most trees have their fruits well along in development; some have completed the process and have dispersed their seeds; but the Basswood is apparently in no hurry and waits until July to come into bloom. But when the time arrives, the floral display which is created seems worth the delay. The manner in which the flowers are borne is rather unique. Each cluster, containing about a dozen flowers, hangs suspended at the end of a stalk which appears to be a free diverging branch from the midrib of an oblong leaf-like bract.

The fruits which follow the flowers often remain, with the bracts, attached to the tree through the winter.

BASSWOOD

Flower

BASSWOOD. AMERICAN LINDEN
Tilia americana L.

LINDEN FAMILY   TILIACEAE

The flowers of the Basswood are creamy white in color, sometimes almost yellow. The five sepals, though somewhat smaller than the petals, have much the same form, and the two sets of parts might be interchanged in position without greatly altering the appearance of the flower. The stamens exhibit a condition found in no other native trees, except members of the Basswood family. They are numerous but occur in five groups, each group being united to a petal-like scale that stands just in front of the true petal. In addition to the general feature just mentioned, each stamen filament is forked at the top, the two branches bearing a half anther each. Almost submerged among the stamens, the pistil consists of a globose ovary with an erect columnar style and a five-lobed stigma.

The fruit is a woody nutlet, attaining the size of a large pea, and on ripening, turns from green to light brown.

HERCULES' CLUB

Portion of Flower-Cluster
HERCULES' CLUB
Aralia spinosa L.

GINSENG FAMILY   ARALIACEAE

There is hardly a feature of the Hercules' Club that does not appear unusual among the trees of our eastern flora. The trunk of the tree is never much branched, though it may attain a height of over thirty feet; young trees are often not branched at all. It is beset with short, sharp spines. The twice-compound leaves are large, sometimes being three or four feet in length and half as wide. Not the least extraordinary feature of the plant is the flower-cluster. Appearing in mid or late summer, great groups of these crown the ends of stems. The individual cluster, often equalling the leaf in length, is twice branched, the numerous branches standing out at right angles from their main axes. All the branches bear whorls of flowers, but only the flowers of the whorls at the ends of primaries ever bloom. One of these whorls is shown in the plate. The color of the flowers is white, with a tinge of green. The corolla falls the day after opening, but for a long time afterward the plant seems to be still in flower, for the clusters retain the same general appearance, largely because of the persistence of the flowers which do not open.

[414]

FLOWERING DOGWOOD

Flower-Cluster
FLOWERING DOGWOOD
Cornus florida L.

DOGWOOD FAMILY   CORNACEAE

With the possible exception of the Magnolias and the Rhododendron, the Flowering Dogwood is probably more famous for its flowers than any other tree of eastern United States. Yet the true flowers of this tree are practically never recognized by anyone except trained students of plant life. The reason for this is that they are small and individually inconspicuous. But each cluster of them is surrounded by a great involucre, consisting of four white, pinkish, or sometimes rose-colored bracts; the effect of the whole inflorescence with its associated structures is that of a flower with a large corolla, and by most observers it is assumed to be such. The Flowering Dogwood has a peculiarly advantageous way of displaying its spring charms. Its favorite habitat is a hillside slope or the bank of a watercourse, and the tendency of the tree to spread its branches out in wide, flat layers, makes for maximum effectiveness.

In fruit, the tree is scarcely less showy than in flower.

ALTERNATE-LEAFED DOGWOOD

Flower
FLOWERING DOGWOOD
Cornus florida L.

DOGWOOD FAMILY   **CORNACEAE**

The true flowers of the Dogwood are usually regarded by the uninformed as being the essential parts of a single large showy flower. But an examination of these parts shows that all the structures of a complete flower are present in each one. It follows, therefore, that the thing which is ordinarily called a flower is really a cluster of flowers, and that the parts generally believed to be petals are really showy bracts which are merely accessory to the flower-cluster.

The calyx is narrowly tubular, and the sepals of which it is composed are evidenced only by four minute teeth on the top of the tube. At full bloom, the four petals are usually strongly reflexed, and the erect stamens protrude well above the corolla rim. The short style stands erect on the center of the ovary, and the latter is encased by the calyx tube.

The fruits, at maturity, are brilliant scarlet in color, and the fruiting phase of the plant is a worthy successor to the flowering stage.

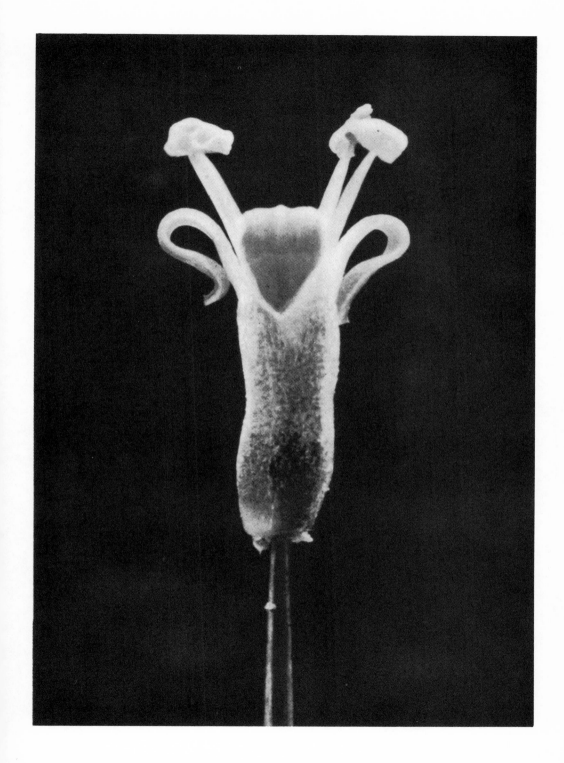

BLACK GUM

Staminate Flower
TUPELO. BLACK GUM
Nyssa sylvatica Marsh.

DOGWOOD FAMILY   **CORNACEAE**

Though sometimes complete, the flowers of the Black Gum are usually either stamen-bearing or pistil-bearing. Both kinds are light green or greenish-white in color and are inconspicuous.

The pistillate occur in few, or several flowered clusters, on short stalks suspended from the axils of leaves of the year. The staminate are borne in the same position, but the clusters are long-stalked and are comprised of numerous flowers. The calyx is tubular, with five small teeth or lobes on the rim. Petals are often lacking altogether, but when present, are minute. Stamens are about ten in number, the filaments differing in length. There is no pistil. Few flowers exhibit to better advantage than this one the structure known as the disk, which is an expansion of the end of the axis to which the flower parts are attached. It appears here as a prominent dome within the cycle of stamens.

GREAT LAUREL

Flower-Cluster
GREAT LAUREL
Rhododendron maximum L.

Those who travel among the eastern mountains of the United States in late June take away with them vivid impressions of the Great Laurel. This plant presents the rather unique case of a form which is rarely called by its common name, but is almost invariably referred to by its scientific designation. The fact that the scientific name of this plant is so commonly used and yet is really harder to pronounce than the average plant name in the Latin, does not fail to present an amusing aspect to the professional botanist, who views almost daily the abhorrence with which the layman regards a scientific name. Here, as in most cases, the classical name is not at all inappropriate, for its meaning is "Rose-tree."

Fully formed the previous September, the great conical and scaly buds from which the flower-clusters develop, open only after the new leaves have expanded. The flowers vary in color, partly with their situation, from white through light rose, to purplish.

The narrow conical fruits may be seen on the branches until the following summer.

MOUNTAIN LAUREL

Flower-Cluster
MOUNTAIN LAUREL
Kalmia latifolia L.

HEATH FAMILY   **ERICACEAE**

The Mountain Laurel is usually shrub-like in habit and size, but it is occasionally a tree. Its period of flowering overlaps that of the Rhododendron, and it is the only rival of the latter at the time of blooming. Some people favor the flowers of the first; others those of the second. Both plants offer supremely beautiful floral displays.

The buds, from which the branched flower-clusters grow, occur in the axils of upper leaves, and during development are overtopped by the new leafy shoots; the flower groups nestle in among the leaves, the rich green of which affords a superb background for the chiefly white flowers.

The fruits are globose, dry capsules, and, topped by the persistent styles, usually remain on their branches until near the next flowering season, constituting a characteristic feature of the plant during the winter and spring.

MOUNTAIN LAUREL

Flower

MOUNTAIN LAUREL

Kalmia latifolia L.

HEATH FAMILY   ERICACEAE

The individual flower of the Mountain Laurel displays a number of interesting features. As soon as the corolla has pushed apart the calyx lobes, and long before it has opened, its ornamental features have begun to appear. At that stage the color is a bright rose. As development progresses one may see the gradual recession of the original hue and the growing dominance of white. The form of the flower also changes radically. At first the corolla is top-shaped, with ten prominent ribs extending to the peak from rounded prominences (pouches) about the periphery; after opening it is cup-like; finally, with full expansion it has the form of a saucer. Now the pouches may be seen holding the anthers of the stamens. In the bud, the stamens were erect and the tips free. But lengthening of the filaments results in carrying the anthers into the recesses of the corolla wall. The spreading of the corolla then bends the stamens outward, until expansion finally releases the anthers, and the elastic filaments suddenly straighten, discharging by centrifugal force the pollen from the open pores at the tips of the pollen sacs.

SOUR-WOOD

Flower

SOUR-WOOD. SORREL-TREE

Oxydendrum arboreum (L.) DC.

HEATH FAMILY   ERICACEAE

The Heath Family contains a wide variety of plant types. A few forms, such as
the Indian Pipe, are leafless parasites; a
few, like the Shin-leaf, are small green
herbs; some, like the Blueberry and the
Leather-leaf, are low tough shrubs; others, such as the Laurel, are sometimes
shrubs and sometimes trees. The only
member of the family, which in the United States, seems to be invariably a tree
in both habit and stature is the Sour-
Wood. Its flowers appear in midsummer,
in linear, one-sided clusters attached to
the terminal portions of the season's
shoots. On each axis the order of flowering is from base to apex and the succession of opening of the flowers in the row
is an interesting one to follow. The individual flowers are urn-shaped, and the
pure white corolla is covered on the exterior by minute hairs. Neither the ten
stamens nor the style is visible from the
exterior unless one peers directly down
the throat of the tube. In fruit, the clusters exhibit the same pattern as when in
flower, except that the individual stalks
become recurved, causing the capsules to
point backward instead of forward along
the main axis.

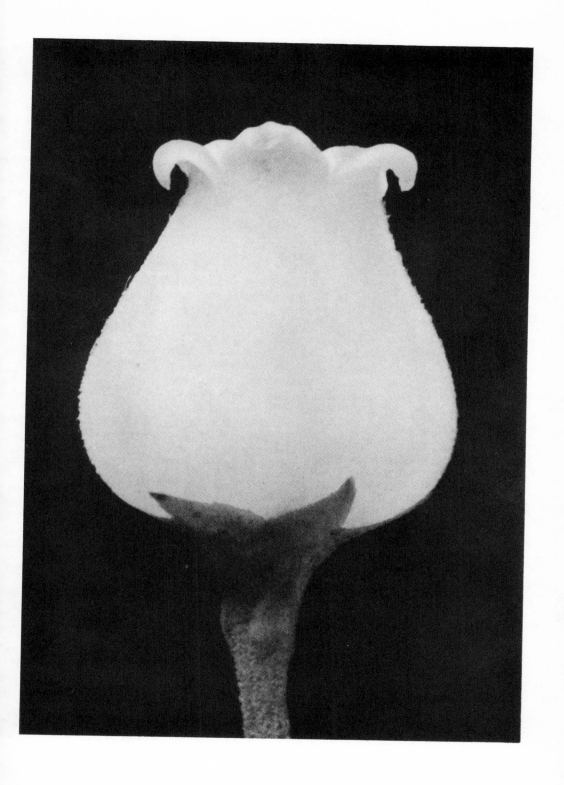

PERSIMMON

Pistillate Flower
PERSIMMON
Diospyros virginiana L.

EBONY FAMILY   EBENACEAE

The Persimmon is better known for its fruit and its wood than for its flowers. Persimmon fruits are famous for their astringent properties when green, and for their lusciousness when ripe. The wood is highly regarded because of its hardness and its resistance to wear. The two kinds of flowers are usually borne on different trees, though occasionally stamens and pistil are produced together. The flowers develop in the axils of leaves of either the current or the past season. The four-lobed calyx is very prominent, and later becomes even larger, persisting as an appendage of the fruit. The pale yellow corolla is variable in form, sometimes being constricted below the reflexed lobes, while in other cases the structure is openly bell-shaped. In the pistillate flower, the stamens, if present at all, are rudimentary; in the staminate flower they are usually sixteen in number, while the pistil is rudimentary or is lacking altogether. The fruits usually ripen only after frost, and may remain on the tree all winter.

SILVER-BELL

Flowers

SILVER-BELL. SNOWDROP
Halesia carolina L.

STORAX FAMILY   STYRACACEAE

The Dogwood blooms so early that the presence of a contender for flowering honors at the time might not be expected, but the Dogwood has a serious rival in the Silver-bell. Not so well known as the Dogwood, because not so widely distributed, the Silver-bell has a charm peculiarly its own. Though the tree in bloom is extremely showy; the term which comes naturally to mind in connection with it is not showiness, but elegance. The flowers, two, three, or four in a cluster, are suspended on individual stalks from the axils of leaves of last year. The green calyx is completely united with the ovary, except for the four minute teeth. The corolla is white, often tinged with rose, and varies widely in the extent to which it is lobed, in the rotundity of profile, and in the degree to which the bell is flared at the open end. The stamens may be as few as eight, or as many as twice that number. The style is straight and slender, and is often of sufficient length to protrude slightly from the bell. When mature, the dry fruit is reddish-brown. It is elongated and two to four winged.

WHITE ASH

Staminate Flower-Clusters
WHITE ASH
Fraxinus americana L.

OLIVE FAMILY   OLEACEAE

The Ashes are important trees with interesting features of form and foliage, but their flowers are among the least interesting. It is true that the floral cluster as a whole may render a pleasing effect in its natural setting, but the individual flowers have little about them in the matter of either form or color that is attractive to the eye. The staminate clusters of the White Ash appear with the opening of the leaf buds, from the axils of last season's leaves. They are fairly compact, even when fully expanded. Supported by a stalk of about its own length, each staminate flower consists of two, or rarely three stamens with long and heavy anthers, but with very short filaments. The calyx is minute and cup-like; a corolla is lacking altogether. At first the stamens are brown-black, but turn reddish-purple, later displaying much yellow, when the pollen sacs open.

[454]

BLACK ASH

Pistillate Flower-Clusters
RED ASH
Fraxinus pennsylvanica Marsh.

OLIVE FAMILY   **OLEACEAE**

Certain of the Ashes produce flowers containing both stamens and pistils; others bear that type of flower only exceptionally, while the White Ash and the Red Ash never exhibit both the essential parts on the same tree. The pistillate clusters of the Red Ash develop from buds of the previous season. The main axis of the cluster stands out stiffly from the twig and the whole inflorescence seems rigid and awkward. In its reduced number of parts, the pistillate flower is similar to the staminate, there being no corolla, and of course, no stamens. The calyx is more deeply cupped than in the staminate flower, and its lobes are longer and more pointed. Completely hidden within the calyx, the ovary sends up its long projecting style which is divided at the apex into two diverging stigmatic lobes.

The dry fruit with its terminal wing is usually taken for a seed. It hangs on the tree until blown off by winter winds.

COMMON CATALPA

Flower-Cluster
COMMON CATALPA
Catalpa speciosa Warder.

BIGNONIA FAMILY   **BIGNONIACEAE**

In bloom, a Catalpa is fully as striking in appearance as the Horse-chestnut. Though the two trees are not closely related, and though their flowers could not be confused, they have in common two striking floral characteristics. One of these is bilateral symmetry, or two-sidedness. In addition to the plant families, to which the Catalpa and the Horse-chestnut belong, only one other represented in these pages displays this type of symmetry; that one being the Legume Family. The other character held in common is color; both flowers are white, with spots of purple and yellow. Aside from the features just mentioned, the two flowers are markedly different. The Catalpa has a tubular corolla which flares widely, almost from its base. At its open end the tube is divided into an upper lip, which is two-lobed, and a lower, which is three-lobed. There are only two stamens, and a simple pistil with a short ovary and a long style. The fruit, the so-called "Indian bean" is a long, dry capsule, which is filled with flat, winged seeds. The tree often displays many of these fruits throughout the winter, and their effect is not a little decorative.

BUTTONBUSH

Flower-Cluster

BUTTONBUSH

Cephalanthus occidentalis L.

MADDER FAMILY   RUBIACEAE

The name Buttonbush would seem to connote a shrubby nature, and over the greater extent of its transcontinental range the plant does fail to attain the proportions of a tree; indeed, in the northern states it is usually only a few feet high. But in the most favorable localities in the South it may reach a height of even fifty feet and possess a trunk measuring a foot in diameter. The favorite habitat of the plant is the low ground of a swamp, or the border of a stream or pond. The creamy-white flowers appear in midsummer and are borne in dense globular heads, each head on a long stalk. This stalk may be the terminal portion of a twig, or one of three branches arising from the base of the terminal stalk, or even one of three branches arising from the axils of the three uppermost leaves. The exactness with which the flowering heads are arranged with reference to the principal axis provides a very neat geometrical pattern, and contributes toward making the Buttonbush a handsome plant when in bloom.

BUTTONBUSH

Flower

BUTTONBUSH

Cephalanthus occidentalis **L.**

MADDER FAMILY   RUBIACEAE

In most inflorescences, or flower-clusters, there is a definite order of blooming.
In some cases the earlier flowers are setting seed before the later flowers open.
But in the Buttonbush, the heads often
seem to mature all the flowers simultaneously, and to exhibit what may be
thought of as one of the most perfect
cases of universal symmetry to be found
among higher organisms.

The individual flower itself is impressive in its slenderness. The calyx tube
encloses and is fused with the ovary. The
corolla tube expands only slightly upward, but the lobes spread in a bell-like
flare. Projecting high above the corolla
is the style of the pistil, crowned by a
prominent stigmatic cap. The four stamens are borne on the throat of the corolla tube, the anthers showing through
the corolla wall just below the notches
between the lobes.

The reddish-brown fruits remain
densely aggregated in heads, and may
often be seen on the plant long after leaf
fall has occurred.

SHEEPBERRY

Flower
SHEEPBERRY. NANNYBERRY
Viburnum Lentago L.

HONEYSUCKLE FAMILY   CAPRIFOLIACEAE

Taken from its setting among the scores of other flowers of the inflorescence, the individual flower of the Sheepberry is, at full development, a handsome object. The green tubular calyx which envelops the ovary is minutely five-lobed at the summit, and supports the five-parted corolla. Five stamens, which seem very large for the flower, are attached to the corolla below the notches. They have been infolded in the bud, but become erect or even spreading, about the time the bright yellow anthers open. The very short style has three stigmatic lobes at the top.

The fruit is blue-black or black in color, and each one in the cluster (most of the flowers fail to set fruit) is attached at the end of a now elongated and red stalk; the plant is as showy in fruit as in flower. The flesh of the fruit, though not copious, is sweet and is often eaten.

[474]

SHEEPBERRY

Portion of Flower-Cluster
SHEEPBERRY. NANNYBERRY
Viburnum Lentago L.

HONEYSUCKLE FAMILY   CAPRIFOLIACEAE

There are, in addition to the dozen shrubby Viburnums of eastern United States, three or four species of the group which reach tree size. Their overlapping geographic ranges cover practically all of the United States east of the plains, and they are similar in vegetative as well as floral features.

The clusters of creamy-white flowers of the Sheepberry are developed from terminal winter buds which may be easily distinguished from those which give rise only to vegetative shoots. The flower buds, while long and pointed, as are the others, exhibit a great enlargement just below the middle; this swelling is due to the presence of the embryo inflorescence within. Flowering occurs after the leaves are well expanded. Sometimes measuring four or five inches across, the flat or slightly convex clusters are produced in such numbers as to load the tree with bloom.

While attractive in appearance, the inflorescence is not more so than the clusters of fruits which ripen early in autumn.

HARD MAPLE

Flower-Clusters
HARD MAPLE
Acer saccharum Marsh.

MAPLE FAMILY   ACERACEAE

Of the larger native Maples, the Sugar Maple and its almost indistinguishable relative the Black Maple, are not only the last to come into flower in the spring, but are also the only ones which develop the flowers simultaneously with the leaves. Late in April or early in May, the floral clusters emerge from terminal leaf buds, or from lateral, leafless buds. The elongation of the slender hairy pedicels outruns the expansion of the leaves; one day the tree seems to be draped in thousands of yellowish-green pendants; only to effect, the next, a quick change to the light green of summer leafage. A well formed Maple tree is pleasing to the eye at any season of the year, but it is especially so at the flowering stage. The tracery of the branches is still as obvious as in winter; but the new lines introduced by the flower pedicels, and the color effect, which is both delicate and fleeting, give a peculiar attractiveness to the tree at this time.

[482]

INDEX

Based on Common Names

[485]

INDEX

Based on Scientific Names

[493]